THE RETURN of JIM RIVERS

NICK & Dan Thompson© 2018

THE RETURN OF JIM RIVERS

CHAPTER 1

Ann Belton sat in the kitchen of the log and adobe ranch house with her Uncle Jesse. They sat at the table, cups of coffee in front of them, looks of despair on their faces. Ann looked over at her Uncle, sad eyes searching his.

"But if we can't get our cattle to market, what is left of them, we are sunk! We just barely have enough money left to live on as it is."I know Chile, times is hard, an' thet damm skunk Sloan is crowdin' us tuh sell.

"We don't have the hands left to make a drive to the railroad Uncle Jesse. The ones that have not been hired away have been scared off. The only two left are Smoky and Wess, and they are getting to be old men. Not able to drive cattle on a long trek. I know that they would fight for me like you would, but I do not want anyone killed over a few cows. Sometimes I think I would be better off to sell out to Jack Sloan, just get it over with. He already has the largest ranch around, and the most hands."

"Sloan is after oure grazing lands Ann. You own the big spring thet feeds Willow Crick, an' thet feeds the grass in this valley keepin' it green. The ranch sets in the mouth uv the valley, an' has the best water in this part of Arizona. Yore daddy knowed thet when he settled hyar, an' got the deed tuh this ranch."

"I wish Dad was here now," Ann whispered sadly, "he would know what to do. He would take care of Sloan and his crew."

"Yeah," Jesse mused," Dave was slick with a gun, an' with his fists too. Which ever wuz called fer. He wuz like thet even when we wuz boys back in Texas. I done good with a gun myself till thet hoss rolled over with me a few years back." He looked at Ann with faded blue eyes," I shore miss yore daddy these days." He shook his head.

Ann reached over and took his gnarled leathery hands in hers." I know if you were able, you would handle Sloan and get our cattle to market."

They set for a long minute like that, each with their own thoughts.

"Uncle Jesse, do you have any ideas about what to do, to get us out of this fix?"

He released her hands, and going to the stove, picked up the coffee pot and refilled their cups. He sat down and took a sip of the hot brew,   then looked at Ann with a twinkle in his eyes.
"Maybe, whut we need around hyar, is a man like Jim Rivers. He could handle thet bunch."

Ann sat back in her chair. Jim Rivers. She had not thought of him for some time. Jim. They had been really close at one time. Almost married in fact. Then Jim had gotten in trouble. They had quarreled, and Jim rode away. Her father had always thought a lot of Jim saying all he needed was a good woman to love him and keep him on the straight and narrow. Her face grew hot as she thought of Jim, and the last time they had been together. There had been a big dance in town that Jim took her to. They danced and laughed most of the night away. Jim had stolen kiss's, begging her to marry him. She had laughed, telling him that he was only a wild boy, too young to be serious about getting married and settling down.

Jim had gotten mad at her for laughing at him. It was a sincere proposal. After she turned him down, he grew aloof and began to drink. She berated him for that, refusing to dance with him anymore that night. By the time the dance had ended, Jim had gotten into two or three fist fights. One fairly serious. Ann refused to let him take her home, and after the dance she went home with Betty Lewis, a good friend of hers.

Next day while doing some shopping at Burkes General Store, she was startled by the sound of gunshots. Going outside she saw a crowd on the wooden sidewalk. Pushing her way through the excited onlookers she gasped, putting her hand over her mouth. Two men lay in the dusty street, one unmoving and still, a gun in his hand, his shirt front bloody where the two bullets had gone through his left shirt pocket. The other man was groaning as he tryed to get up, but kept falling back in the street. Standing facing them was Jim, a smoking Colt six gun in each hand still extended in front of him. There was a bloody splotch on his left side where a bullet had ripped through his shirt. Ann had stood rooted to the sidewalk, her legs weak, and suddenly trembling all over as she reached for a porch post to support her. Jim flipped his six guns and sheathed them as he faced the crowd gathered there.

All of you seen an' heard it," he had called," they accused me of rustlin' an' tryed to cold deck me! It was a fair fight." "Won't make no difference tuh old John Sloan," Sheriff Tom Blaine called out as he stepped off the wood into the street, and stood facing Jim. "Maybe yuh ought tuh make yore self scarce 'round hyar fer a spell. I ain't gonna press no charges again yuh Jim, 'cause I know it wuz a fair fight. I seen it frum across the street. Thing about it is, with one uv his hands dead an' his boy shot up, fair won't matter tuh John 'er none uv the Sloans!"

Jim had looked over then, seeing Ann standing there, frozen in place, a look of horror on her white face. He tipped his hat to her, a grim expression on his pale features, turned on his heel, and walked away. Ann wanted to call out to him, but she couldn't move or speak. Her heart was racing, her mouth was dry, and her tongue clove to the roof of it. Many were the thoughts that raced through her mind then, but she stood speechless not believing what she had just witnessed. Jim was a killer! He had just killed one man and seriously shot another who might die! No! It could not be! But there was the proof, lying in the dusty street before her!

Her mind was in turmoil, confusion, she felt faint. The scene swam before her. Jim couldn't be a cold blooded killer!

But, she saw the two men lying there before her, and Jim standing there with those two black smoking guns in his hands. No, this could not be happening! Was she somehow to blame? Had she driven him to this? She leaned against the porch post placing her trembling hands over her breast to try and stop her throbbing, racing heart.

Suddenly Ann remembered the blood on his shirt as he stood there so strong and fearless facing the crowd. Was he hurt bad? Would she ever see him again? She had to find Jim. To talk with him. To help him. Protect him even, if she could. Her vision cleared, her feet became unstuck, and she started down the street in the direction Jim had disappeared in like someone in a dream. She must face him. Let him know she understood. But she was too late! Jim was riding out of town leaning sideways in his saddle. Too Late! She was too late! Ann tried to call out to him, but the words stuck in her throat. Gone! Jim was gone! She had waited too long to see him! Only a plume of dust hung in the air to show his passing! She turned and slowly plodded back up the street on wooden legs, and leaden feet. Her heart sunk inside her. She had pushed him too far. She had failed him.

Ann came back to the present with a start!" What Uncle Jesse?" I jist asked where yuh wuz. Looked like yuh wuz miles away frum hyar."

Yes, I was. I....was thinking of the last time I saw Jim. How I failed him.""Me too. Yuh took it awful hard, him ridin' away hurt like he wuz.

"Uncle Jess, do you think Jim has turned outlaw?"

"Wal, I would hev tuh say no tuh thet Ann. I hev heard a few stories frum time tuh time aboot Jim. All tuh the good I am glad tuh say." "Ann stared intently at her Uncle." You never told me that."

"No, no I did not."

"Why? Didn't you think I would have liked to have known?" "Wal, I did not know if yuh would hev been interested atall."

"Of course I would have been interested!"

"So, yuh still hev feelin' fer him then?"

"I have never gotten over Jim, uncle, I still love him," she whispered.

Jesse poured him another cup of coffee, settling back in his chair, a glint of humor in his faded blue eyes." When Jim left hyar, he joined up with a trail herd goin' tuh Dodge City. He made thet drive an' wuz foreman on a couple more. Seems like Jim made a name fer hisself on them drives. After thet he hunted buffalo, an' fer a while wuz a shotgun guard on the Wells-Fargo stage line. Last I heard uv him, he was the marshall uv a town up south uv hyar. Maybe still is."

Jesse saw by the expression on his niece's face that he had her full undivided attention. Her face glowed, she seemed mesmerized by his story of Jim. There was a knowing look about him as he watched her face.

"Want me tuh see if I kin git in touch with him Ann," he smiled? She sat lost in thought for a few minutes. Jesse sipped his coffee, rolled a smoke and waited with that knowing smile on his face.

Ann spoke slowly, choosing her words." Yes. If you can locate him, tell him that I need him. That I am in deep trouble and need him badly. Also, tell him I have a business proposal to offer that will please him, tell him I still love him, have waited for him."This last was said with a slight flush on her face, her eyes dark, a soft expression in them. An expression of love and remembrance of days gone past.

Next morning as the sun was peeking over the hills, Jesse was on his way into Rimrock. In his pocket was Ann's message to be sent to Jim Rivers if he could be located. Jesse smiled to himself. If Jim could be located, if he would come, things were soon to change around here. Ann seemed like his daughter more so than a niece being he had never been married. Dave had been his only brother, and he had no other kinfolks but her. He just wanted to see her happy, and settled with a good husband before they laid him to rest.

CHAPTER 2

Almost two weeks after Jesse sent the telegram, a tall young man rode into Rimrock, down the dusty main street looking neither left nor right. He was astride a coal black, proud stepping Stallion. The horse matched the man astride him for rugged, trail weary, dusty appearance. He drew rein in front of the Red Horse Saloon. Stepping from the saddle in one lithe movement he flipped the reins over the hitchrail and stepped upon the boardwalk. His cool gray eyes took in every detail as he looked the town over. He wore a black, flat topped hat, red shirt, black jeans, and high topped boots with silver Mexican spurs. Two dark walnut handled .44 Colts hung at his sides within easy reach of his long fingers. Another Colt was tucked behind his belt at his back, and a twelve inch razor sharp Bowie knife hung under his left arm. Two rifle sheaths showed on his horse. The one in the front of the saddle on the right side holding a .44-40 Henry, the other on the left side under the saddle skirt and a little behind contained a .50 caliber Sharps. He was outfitted for a war and looked like he could win one. He saw three other horses tied at the hitching rack, all wearing the Box S brand. It was food for thought. Taking off his hat, he dusted his pants and shirt. Settling it back on his head, he pushed open the batwing doors, stepped quickly through and to one side, letting his eyes adjust to the dark interior of the barroom. He placed everyone there in one sweeping glance. There were three cowhands standing at the bar drinking and laughing. Four other men sat at a corner table playing poker. He crossed the room, his spurs jingling, to stand with his left side against the bar. A stout man with slicked down hair and red sleeve garters came down the bar toward him.

"What kin I git yuh stranger," he asked in a coarse voice?

"A shot of your best Rye and a cool beer," answered the stranger in a mild voice.

The bartender filled a shot glass from a brown bottle, sat it in front of him, then turned to fill a mug with beer. A coin dropped on the bar and the bartender scooped it up putting it in the till. He turned back to the stranger.

"Come far?"

"Pretty far, yes."

"Well looks like you come well armed," the bartender returned.The stranger gave a bleak smile as the bartender moved away, wiping at the bar top with a half clean rag. The stranger sipped the beer. It was fairly cold and had a good taste. He took the shot of Rye and threw it down noticing as he did that he was getting his fair share of attention from the trio of cowboys at the far end of the bar. One of them seemed awfully interested in him. He sipped his beer, waiting. It would come, it always did.

The red faced cowboy poured another drink from the bottle near his hand, and tossing it down, wiped his mouth on the back of his hand, giving the stranger a baleful stare. He stepped away from the bar and called out in a drunken voice; " Hey stranger, don't I know yuh? Cold gray eyes looked him over."No."

The cowboy reached for the bottle again, poured a drink and said something over his shoulder to his friends. They laughed. He got a little louder. "Seems like tuh me, thet a man with all them guns must be scared uv somethin'"

He stepped farther up the bar to peer directly at the tall stranger. Yuh scared uv somethin' er somebody stranger?"

The man in the black hat and tied down guns just looked at the drunken cowboy wanting to brace him. He gave a deep sigh.

"Not so's you would notice," he said in a soft cool voice.

"Wal I think yuh aire," and the drunken cowboy took another step closer to the stranger, his hands helt away from his body.

Everything got so still you could hear the clock ticking behind the bar. The men playing poker at the corner table laid their cards down, watching the drama unfolding before them. The other two cowboys eased farther down the bar away from their friend. One of them said something to him, but was waved away.

"I have no quarrel with you boy," the stranger said, his hands hanging loosely by his sides.

"Jist maybe I got one with yuh."

"It does not have to be like this."

"I knowed yuh wuz jist a big bluff when I seen yuh come in with all them guns, trying tuh look like a gunman. Whar yuh frum?"

"All over."

"All over huh. Ever hear uv me? Folks call me the Sundown Kid. Thet's 'cause when men come up again me, it's sundown fer them!" "Can't say I have ever heard of you, nor have I seen any of your graveyards either."

The men at the table laughed, and the Sundown Kid threw them a malovent glare, his right hand twitching.

"Ah, a smart ass hombre huh. Wal right hyar is where I put another notch on my gun. Big bad gunman, baw. Haw haw haw! You might never hev heard uv me before, but thet don't matter, cause after today yuh won't know nothin', ever again!"

The stranger took another sip of his beer; "What are you goin' to do, talk me to death?"

This remark brought another round of laughter, even the bartender joining in. The four card players drew another dark glare from the KId.

"Yore big mouth is digging you a grave big gun fighter," the Kid hissed. I do not wear these guns for show boy."

The Kid seemed to spring forward, his hands curling into claws as he bent forward slightly, his red rimmed eyes shooting sparks.

"I ain't no boy as yuh aire goin' tuh find out in a minute. That is 'lessen yuh aire afraid tuh drag iron again a real gunman," the Kid roared! The stranger blew out a disgusted sigh. "Well boy, if nothin' else will do you, turn your wolf loose."

His icy gray eyes bored into this cowboy, this Sundown Kid, this blowhard full of whiskey, this wanna be gunman, this dyed in the wool fourflusher.

The Kid licked his suddenly dry lips. This stranger did not seem to be impressed with who he was at all. Did not seem to be nervous or afraid. In fact he seemed to be bored by the whole thing. His eyes darted left and right. He was alone! All alone with this cool acting stranger whose cold eyes were boring into him. Sweat broke out on his clammy brow. The raw whiskey he had been drinking rolled in his stomach and he had a sour taste in his mouth. Someone would stop it! Surely they would! Had he taken the thong off his pistol? Maybe his pistol would hang in its holster. What if it did? He wiped his sweaty palms on his pants legs. The four men at the corner table sat looking at him, waiting for him to make his move. He had run his mouth, now he had to back it up. The stranger wore a disgusted look on his face. As if tired of waiting for him to make a move, he reached for his beer with his left hand and took another sip.

The Sundown Kid seeing his chance, grabbed for his gun. It slid out of it's greased holster into his hot hand. He grinned as it came up. He would show them! The stranger waited till the Kid had his pistol out before he drew. He drew and fired so fast, his arm was a blur, the bullet taking the Kid in the shoulder. His gun clattered to the floor as he grabbed his shoulder, and stood there stupidly, staring at the blood leaking between his fingers, and dripping to the floor. The stranger punched the empty shell out and fed a fresh one into the chamber, his eyes on the Kid's two companions, but they stood stock still. He flipped his gun and it settled into it's holster.

"You boys best take your friend to the doctor before he bleeds to death," he spoke quietly into the silent room.

He looked around the saloon, finished his beer then made his way out the door behind the two men taking the Sundown Kid to the doctor for patching up. As he mounted his stallion and rode slowly away, a babble of talk broke out behind him. Other people hearing the gunshot, and seeing him ride away came in off the street to find out what went on.

"Did yuh see thet hombre draw?"

"Too fast fer me tuh foller."

"Who in the Hell wuz he anyway?"

"Dont know who he wuz, but he shore put his brand on the Sundown Kid."

One of the men who came in was the Sheriff, Tom Blaine. The men gathered there looked over at him.

"Do you know who he wuz Sheriff?"

"I do. Usted tuh know him quite well in fact", he replied in a soft drawl."Wal, kin yuh tell us who he wuz?"

"Fellars, thet wuz Jim Rivers, an' where ever he is, action follers." "Jim Rivers. I thought he looked familar," one said.

"Thet wild gunman frum Dodge City, friend uv Bill Hickcock,"

another asked?"I remember when Jim left hyar after a shootin', an' helped take a herd up the trail tuh Dodge."

"Yeah, thet next trip he shot it out with the Banner gang when they tryed tuh cut his herd."

"He is the one that killed John Shipley when he wuz Marshall uv Bittercreek."

The Sheriff stood and listened to the excited talk around him. Storys were told and retold over drinks, but all had the same thought on their minds, what was Jim Rivers doing back in these parts? Of them all, the Sheriff was the only one who had an idea why he was here. Ann Beldon was having a hard time with the Sloans, and somewhere in the equation, Jim Rivers figgered into it. He stood by quietly, smoking and having a small drink with the men there as he figgered on things. He knew a lot about Jim Rivers, for he had kept up with him over the years. In fact, he was the one who kept Ann's Uncle Jesse up to date on Jim, as Jesse cared for Ann and Jim, he wanted them to have another chance at love. A slight smile touched his lips, his gray eyes crinkling at the corners. He knew Jim's family well. His father had been the town's Blacksmith, and his mother a school teacher. They were caught out in a flash flood and drowned when Jim was ten. It had hit Jim hard, and he grieved for months. Tom Blaine and his wife had no children of their own, so they took him in and helped raise him, along with Dave Belton, who gave him his first riding job. He knew Jim to be honest and fearless, also he was good with a gun. If he took a hand in Ann's trouble with the Sloans, things would pick up real quick. Damm, he liked that boy. Turning on his heel, he walked back to his office as a weight seemed to be lifted off his chest. Jesse and Dave Belton and JIm's father and Tom had been friends ever since they settled here. Tom had never cared much for the Sloans. They were a wild, rough, unruly bunch, but being Sheriff, he couldn't do much unless there was a killing in the county. He kept a tight rein on the doings in town, and everybody heeded his warnings, for Tom Blaine was a tough man, and a good hand with a gun himself. Now Jim Rivers was back. An idea was forming in the back of his head. Things would change. Tom liked that cute little Ann Belton too.

CHAPTER 3

Ann was out in the yard when she saw the rider coming down the lane. There was something familiar about the way he sat his horse. As he drew closer, she shaded her eyes to get a better look at the tall rider. Was it Jim? It looked like him from where she stood. Uncle Jesse told her he had sent the telegram after talking to Sheriff Blaine. When she saw it was Jim for certain, tears dimmed her eyes. He stopped a few feet away and slid from the saddle to stand gazing at her from under his wide hat brim. Ann's hands flew to her breast, to clutch tightly there.

"Jim, it is you," she whispered in a soft tearful voice! Her hands flew to her hot face. "Jim," she said again, tears staining her cheeks. The name came out breathlessly, as if she could get no air in her lungs. Her heart pounded in her chest as though it would jump out." You came!"

He dropped his reins. "Yes Ann, I came."

She stared at him through her tear dimmed eyes, holding out shaking hands to him. "Yes, you came. Thank you Jim."

He clasped her cold hands in his big warm ones. "Your telegram said it was urgent." He looked at her, questions on the tip of his tongue."Yes, yes, it is urgent Jim. Let's go into the house and I will tell you all about it."

Holding onto his hand, her head reaching the top of his shoulder, as they walked toward the house side by side, she could hardly believe it was Jim, her Jim! Seating him at the big kitchen table, she poured coffee for the two of them and took a seat across from him, forming her words in her mind.

"Where to start. I suppose it all began to happen after Dad got killed in the stampede a year ago this month."

"What? Your father is gone? Dave is dead?"

They were gathering the cattle for a drive when they were stampeded by some masked men. Anyway, Dad was out front when his horse stumbled, throwing him, and the cattle ran over him. After that, everything around here started going downhill. Cows rustled, hands ran off, shots taken at Uncle Jesse. Just one thing after another." "Did you go to the Sheriff?"

"Yes. Tom came out and investigated. He had his suspicions, but no proof that would hold up in court. He has been working on that ever since it happened. Jack Sloan has been trying to buy me out since Dad died. You remember him. You shot his brother in town that fateful day you rode away from me.

Jim's eyes flashed." It seemed like at the time you wanted nothin' to do with me."

"Yes, it seemed that way, but I was a young foolish girl then. Did you know I ran after you that day, trying to catch up with you, to see how badly you were hurt?"

"No, I did not. But I never blamed you Ann. I had some growing up to do, an' I have done it over the years.

"I have also grown up since then Jim. I am no longer a young foolish girl. Now I am a woman. You see, I have grown up too. Do you forgive me for what happened then?

He smiled, looking into her soft brown eyes." There is nothin' to forgive Ann. You have been in my mind an' dreams ever since I left." "You have never had a girlfriend, someone to share your thoughts and dreams with while you were gone?"

"No, never. I had no time for girlfriends where I was. Always on the go. Never knowin' when someone would shoot me in the back, or meet a faster gun. I have lived a rough life since I left here Ann. But I always knew I would come back here to you."

Her eyes searched his, knowing he spoke the truth.

"Anyway, John Sloan has been in bad health for some time now. Jack, his oldest son has been running the ranch for the past two years, and he is tougher than the old man ever was. Mean, sneaky, brags a lot. He used to come here wanting to take me to dances and the like, but I always turned him down. His brother Bill is the Ramrod, and in some ways is worse than Jack. Mark, the one you shot, has been in a wheelchair since the shooting. They are a bitter, harsh, cruel family.""How many riders do they have?"

"All told, about fifteen or so. A rough bunch. Jack Sloan comes by every so often to make me an offer on the ranch. The last time he was here with Bill, he asked me to marry him."

Jim gave out a loud snort.

"He says that is the only way out for me to save the ranch. To tell you the truth, I have about given up. We can't get the cattle to market because we don't have enough hands. With Rimrock being twelve miles away, I can't just run in to the Sheriff every time something happens. No one will work here because they are afraid of the Sloans."Jim nodded his head, "I see your problem Ann."

"There is no way to drive our cattle to market because we have been black listed. Uncle Jesse, Wess, and Smoky are all good men, but they are old men, not able to face up to a wild bunch like the Sloans, even though they would try for me. Also, our cattle are disappearing. Uncle Jesse says it is rustlers."

Lighting a long slim Cigar, Jim looked at her through the blue smoke as she continued her story.

"I have been at my wits end lately trying to keep body and soul together. Our money in the bank is almost gone. Old Fred Burke gives me credit at his store, and said he would carry me as long as needed. I was ready to give up and sell out Jim, when I thought of you. If you ever cared anything for me at all, maybe you will help me, my old friend and childhood sweetheart," she finished in a low whisper.

The pleading, searching look in her tear filled eyes was almost more than Jim could bear. That look from her dark brown eyes took him back, and the last few years melted away as if they never were. He reached across the table and took her cold shaking hands, smiling at her. Rejection. I....I was not sure you would come after the way we parted," she whispered, tears streaming down her cheeks." After the way I treated you that night, I would not have blamed you at all if you had not come."
He squeezed her cold hands." All you had to do was let me know you were in trouble, an' I would have come runnin'. I would do anything for you Ann, you know that."

"Oh Jim," she cryed, pulling her hands away from his, covering her tear stained face with them. Her hot tears leaked through, dripping down softly. She was saved from farther embarrassed by the arrival of Jesse. His face lit up like the rising sun at the sight of Jim setting there. He came around the table with outstretched hand, and Jim got up to meet it with his in a firm handshake.

"Howdy old timer."

"Jim! Good tuh see yuh boy," he replied with his face wreathed in a happy grin." Has Ann told yuh oure sad story?"

"Most of it Jesse," Jim answered as he walked to the stove to refill his coffee cup. Turning, he said, "just you three left huh?"

"Thets right Jim, Smoky, Wess, an' me."

"How many head of cattle?"

"Rough count, about fifteen, sixteen hunerd, down frum three thousand. Two maybe two fifty head uv breedin' stock left. Somehow we hev been able tuh hold on tuh them by stayin' in the saddle day and night. But we keep 'em in close."

"So, they are rustlin' the cattle, an' keepin' you from drivin' to market.""Thet is jist about the size uv it Jim," Jesse replied, scratching his white head.

"Hev yuh told him what yuh hev in mind Ann," asked her Uncle?"No, not yet Uncle Jesse, "she returned, her face growing beet red.Jesse grinned and winked at her."Wal, I will git an' let yuh young folks talk it over." Still grinning he closed the door softly behind him.

"Talk what over," Jim asked?

Ann helt his eyes with hers; "Remember that proposition I mentioned in my telegram Jim?"

He nodded, his mind wondering.

"I have told you all that has happened here since you have been gone. Uncle Jesse, bless him, is too old and crippled up to hold this ranch for me against an outfit like the Sloans. I need a strong man to help me here. Someone who can handle cattle, and men. A man I know I can trust."

She studied his face as she talked, her face white as marble, her bossom heaving. "A man I have strong feelings for. I need you Jim. You can hold this ranch for us. You can get our cattle to market. You can stand against the Sloans. You Jim, I need you. I need your help Jim, desperately."

She took his shirt in her hands and pressed her soft warm body again him, looking at him with all the power of her woman's nature, her white face close to his.

"And now, I will tell you the proposition I have in mind, if you will accept it. It will take a strong man like you to do this, and I will not insult you by offering you wages. I want you to be my partner. Yes, partner in more ways than one Jim. I offer you my love forever, my soul, my all. I love you Jim. I have always loved you, but was too blind to see it in time to keep you from going away. But now I know Jim darling, I love you, and want you to be my husband! She finished in a soft whisper, swaying against him, her face on fire from the bold statement she had just uttered to the man she loved.

"What? Husband?"

"Yes, my husband. Don't you remember that night long ago when you asked me to marry you?"

"Yes I do. And I remember your answer too."

Ann became flustered. Her hands fluttered like butterflies, her face suddenly as white as chalk, her soft brown eyes wide. "But I was only a girl then Jim, just seventeen, and you were only eighteen. We were just kids. That was five years ago, and I am a woman now, with a woman's feelings and needs. By marrying me, we will own this ranch together Jim. You and me, and maybe someday, our children will own it."She reached out shaking hands to him, and he took them in a firm grip."I thought of you all the time Ann. I knew someday I would come back an' marry you, but not until I had proven myself."

"I have thought of you too Jim, a lot over the years. Uncle Jesse only told me a little while back what you had been doing the past years. I think he knew it all along. How you were a man other men respected and trusted. Now, I am putting my faith and trust in you Jim. Will you be my partner, my......my husband?" Her flushed face reddened even more.

Jim gripped her hands. "Yes Ann, I will be your partner, an' I would be proud to make you my wife. I will bust this range wide open. I will make sure you an' our ranch will be safe!"

He released her hands, drawing her close to him. He could feel her heart pounding against his chest. "I recon a kiss will seal the deal," he told her with a wide smile.

Their lips met in a warm, long, deep kiss that felt good to both of them. He kissed her lips, her flushed cheeks, her throat, and her eyes, lavishing upon her all the hunger of the long lonely years he had been away. She responded to his kiss's with several of her own. Finally, with a long shuddering breath, Jim pulled away from her, only to hug her tight again. Ann lay her glossy head upon his shoulder, tears leaking through her tightly closed eyes. Jim was back. She was safe..

CHAPTER 4

Breakfast two mornings later was a festive occasion. Jesse, Smoky and Wess made merry over the young couple. Ann was mostly silent wearing a big smile, but Jim traded banter with them. After eating and the dishes cleaned up, Ann went into her bedroom to change while the men went outside. Soon they were settled in the shiny black Buckboard, with a team of matched grays in the traces. "I will keep a eye on thet black uv yore's while yuh aire gone Jim," Smoky volunteered, "he is shore one fine piece uv hossflesh."

"Thanks Smoky. He is a fine animal, the best horse I ever owned.""Wal, yuh young folks better git movin'" Jesse told them." Yuh hev got a long day ahead of yuh. Don't take long tuh git hitched, but it shore takes a long time tuh git ready fer it," he laughed, along with Wess and Smoky. He winked at Ann, giving her a fond look.

Ann blushed to the roots of her dark brown hair, as Jim picked up the reins, and made ready to start.

"We will be back tomorrow boys, then we will make war talk. Stay close to the ranch while we are gone," and with a flourish of the reins, flicked the horses into motion.

The grays seemed glad to be out today, and pulled the buggy along at an easy trot. They talked little on the ride into Rimrock. Jim seemed deep in thought, and Ann seemed nervous, for after all, it was her wedding day. She would be married to a man she hadn't seen in five years. But they had always been close, even when he was a young, wild cowboy riding for her father. He was kind and gentle when they were young, and he was the same man now, only older, steadier, wiser. She knew that she had done the right thing, sending for Jim and marrying him. Jim remembered himself, asking her a lot of questions on the nature of people around here now, range conditions, and who was losing cattle. Ann told him everything she knew, or had heard of the things he asked about, and soon they were in town. The trip into town took over two hours in a buckboard and longer in a wagon. As Jim helped her down from the buckboard at the livery stable, Ann looked in dismay at her dusty clothes.

"Give them a good feed after you rub them down," Jim told

the stable man, an old fellow with a limp.

"Howdy Miss Ann," the old man smiled, "an' you too Jim Rivers. Jim took a longer look at the old man.

"Hello Mose," Ann replied sweetly.

Then recognition came to Jim." Mose Everhart," he exclaimed. "I did not reconize you behind all them whiskers! How have you been?" Shaking the old man's hand warmly, he turned to Ann." Mose taught me how to ride and care for horses. I was just a snott nosed kid, but he took me under his wing and taught me all the things I know today about horses."

"Mose, I figgured you would be on the front porch in a comfortable rocker by now."

"My grandson runs the place, I jist like tuh hang around hyar with him."

"I was sorry to hear about Mike," Jim said, shaking his head.

Mose looked at him out of watery blue eyes." Yeah, thanks Jim. He loved drivin' thet stage fer Wells-Fargo. Bandits helt up the stage one day an' shot Mike out of the seat. No need fer it. He wouldna' drawed on 'em. Killed the shotgun guard too. Didn't want tuh leave any witness's I suppose. They wasn't even carryin' no strong box. All the bandits got wuz a sack uv mail. Damm shame."

He looked up at the blue sky for a minute, swallowing hard." Like tuh uv killed his Ma when she heard it. He wuz our only child. But Mike's widder an' Tim, their son live with us now. Thet helps some fer Pearl. Gives her somebody tuh fuss over.

Jim lay a caring hand on Mose's shoulder. "Tell Pearl I am comin' over one day soon, an' have her bake me a apple pie like she usted to when me an' Mike was kids together."

Mose laughed, "thet would tickle her plum pink Jim. I heahed yuh wuz back, an' left yore mark on thet Sundown Kid thets been a roaring around here. Now thet yuh aire back, gonna stay a while?"

JIm pulled Ann closer to him." Yes I am Mose. Back for good, cause me an' Ann are gettin' married today."

Mose's mouth fell open as he stared at them." Wal, fer the land sakes. Married."

"Yeah, I am going to run the Rocking B for me an' Ann."

A happy look shone in Mose's faded blue eyes." Good. Good. I am glad fer the both uv yuh. He smiled at Ann," yuh got yuh a good man Miss Ann."She nodded as she smiled back, "I know Mose, I know." Stepping closer to Jim after glancing around, Mose said in a low voice," watch yerself son, Jack Sloan an' Snap Winters aire in town. Thet Sundown Kid is usualy with 'em, but he is laid up jist now," giving Jim a broad wink.

Jim gave him a friendly pat on the shoulder," thanks Mose. Take care."Taking Ann's elbow in his left hand, he escorted her up to Burke's store.

"Ann, I want you to buy you a weddin' dress an' anything else you want that takes your fancy while I am gone."

"JIm," she asked fearfully?"

"No, "he smiled, "I am just goin' over an' have a talk with Tom Blaine. Won't be gone long, just go on with your shoppin'. I will be back soon."Ann watched his tall form walk out the door. The way he paused and looked up and down the street before he stepped out into it. Even on his wedding day he wore his twin Colts.

Tom Blaine looked up from reading a wanted poster when Jim entered. He rose from behind his desk with outstretched hand.

"Jim," he said warmly, "good tuh see yuh son. Have a seat an' make yore self tuh home. Yuh look good fer a ole star packer."

"Thanks Tom. It is good to see you too. How's things around?"

"Wal, little rustlin', little stealin', the usual."

"Did you get the telegram I sent you Tom?"

The Sheriff nodded his shaggy head." Yeah, got it about two weeks after I sent mine."

They talked for almost half an hour, and when Jim got up to leave, he had a fair idea about some things that were on his mind.

"Want tuh have a drink with me Jim, "Tom asked?"

"I would like to Tom, but Ann and I are gettin' married today, guess I better not."

Tom's eyebrows shot up, "Married? Why, yuh jist got hyar."

"I know, but it has been comin' for years, an' I want you to be my best man."

"Yeah, I remember son. Wal, I will be there with bells on. Married after two days in town. Wal, wal," Tom said with a big grin on his weathered face.

When he got back to Burkes Store, Fred told him that Ann had bought a dress along with some other things, and was gone over to Betty Miller's house to get ready. He shook Jim's hand wishing them well. Ann left word that he could pick her up there. Betty Miller was Ann's old friend, Betty Lewis. Before Jim left the store, he bought Ann a set of rings, plus a new black suit for himself. Paying Fred, he went down to the barber shop for a bath, shave and haircut. When he was finished, he rolled his old clothes into a bundle and tied them with a piggin string. Then he walked over to Betty's to collect Ann. Betty answered the door with a big smile on her face.

"Come in Jim, she is ready and waiting."

As Jim walked into the spacious house, a small boy of about three came out of the kitchen eating a biscuit, a wooden gun clasped in his other hand. Jim looked at Betty.

"Yes, he is mine," she told Jim as she picked the boy up. This is Dan Miller Junior.

"Dan Miller. I remember him, worked at the express office."

"Yes. He is the manager there now."

"Favors his father. Congratulations Betty."

"You too," she whispered. "Ann," she called," your beau is here and looking handsome too."

Ann came into the room slowly, gazing at Jim, a radiant smile on her pretty face. Jim stared at her as a big grin crawled across his tanned face. He gave a low whistle. A white gown shimmered on her, and a light blue silk shawl covered her shoulders. Her hair was done up in layers, the reddish brown tint matching her shining eyes. Jim stared at her, overcome by her beauty.

"Ann, you are beautiful he said in a hushed voice."

Her smile got wider," thank you Jim."

Betty's mother came in then, a sparkle in her eyes. "What do you think of your bride Jim?"

He shook his head," I shore am a lucky man."

"The preacher is waiting on you," she told him, " I have already made all the arrangements for you."

He bowed to her." Thank you Missus Lewis."

Jim helt out his hand and Ann floated over to him as he took her arm."Oh, a new suit. You don't look too bad yourself," she laughed. The remark made Jim feel a little uncomfortable, but he grinned. "Betty is going with us Jim, she is going to be my maid of honor." He nodded." I asked Tom Blaine to stand up with me. Said he would meet us at the Church."

As they approached the little white Church, Tom Blaine and his wife stood on the steps waiting. He smiled at Ann.

"Never saw yuh looking prettier Ann."

"Thank you Tom," she said nervously.

Tom's wife, Ruth hugged her then turned to Jim." It is so good to see you again Jim," and she gave him a big hug and kiss.

Inside the Church were several of the townspeople that knew the young couple, that was a surprise to Jim. The preacher, standing at the front waved them forward. His wife sat at the old pump organ on a swivel stool, hands poised over the keys. Jim and Tom took off their gunbelts, hanging them on a peg by the door. The organ began to play as they walked up the isle to the altar. Tom stood by Jim's side, and Betty beside Ann. The preacher opened his worn Bible and it began.Soon the service was over. Jim and Ann were now husband and wife. Ann stared at the matching set of rings on her finger. They were married.

"You may now kiss your bride," the preacher said as he winked at Jim.Outside, the small crowd gathered around them, and the newlyweds went off with good wishes ringing in their ears. Before they left, Jim stuck a ten dollar bill in the preacher's hand and the preacher nodded his thanks.

As they walked into town, Jim looked up at the sun.

"Gettin' married shore does make a man hungry," he said. "Tom, if you an' Ruth an' Betty will go with us to the hotel, I will buy supper." "I am gittin' kinda lank myself," Tom told him, laying his arm across his wife's shoulder, "we could eat."

"let me run down to the express office and get Dan, and we will take supper with you too," Betty spoke up.

"Go ahead Betty, I will get a table while we are waitin',"Jim told her. They marched into the hotel lobby, and on into the large dining room. The hotel served a good meal. You could get most anything there. They found a corner table that would accommodate them all and sat down. In a few minutes Betty and Dan came in. Dan congratulated them as he sat down. The waitress came over and they settled on steaks, green beans, mashed potatoes, apple pie and coffee. The supper was good as always, and they sat over coffee talking. Soon Tom stretched his arms announcing that it was time for him to make his rounds. Betty and Dan had to get home to their son and the party broke up. They left and Jim and Ann sat alone, talking quietly. They stood to leave and Jim left the girl who waited on them a dollar tip. At the hotel desk Jim announced to the clerk," we want the best room in the house for the night."

"Yessir. Sign here," and he turned the register book around so Jim could sign it.

Jim registered as Mr and Mrs Jim Rivers in a bold hand. Ann blushed becomingly as she read it. Mrs Jim Rivers. She turned a lovely face to Jim. He smiled at her as she turned the golden ring on her hand.

"I have butterflys in my stomach," she told Jim.

"No reason to be nervous, but then a woman don't get married every day to a man she ain't seen in five years."

"Betty told me that she felt the same way the day she and Dan got married."

Jim patted her arm, and gave her a warm smile, but something was on his mind. At supper, a man had sat at a table near a window watching them. He wore two tied down guns and had a white puckered scar across his left cheek. He had seemed to be very interested in the newly married couple. Jim had spotted him as soon as he entered the dining room and took a seat so he could face him. Tom had also noticed him sitting there. After a while, the man got up, paid his bill and walked outside. He stared at them through the window for a few moments, then mounted a dark bay horse riding south out of town.

Jim slipped the clerk some money and told him to bring a bottle of Champagne up to their room. He escorted Ann through the lobby, where she drew many admiring glances, up the stairs to their room. He unlocked the door, and sweeping her up in his arms, carried her into the fancy decorated room. Sitting her on her feet, they exchanged a long kiss. A knock on the door signaled the arrival of their Champagne. The clerk sat the bucket on a small table by two comfortable chairs, and Jim gave him a dollar. Opening the bottle and pouring each a glass, Jim sat down in one of the chairs and began to talk about the years he had been gone. The long trail drives, the dust, sweat, and long hours in the saddle, gunfights, the lonely rides, indians, drought, lack of water, the scant meals, but most of all the deep lonesome feelings inside. Missing something, needing something, and not knowing just what it was.

"But now I know what it was I missed," he said looking at her sweet face as he covered her hand with his.

"And what was that Jim?"

"A woman's love. Someone to care for you, to walk beside you, and most of all, to have a home where she will be waiting."

Ann's eyes grew misty as he talked." I will always love you and be home waiting for you Jim," she promised.

CHAPTER 5

Outside the sun was sinking as they sat talking about their future together. Soon lamps were being lit all over town, and Jim lit the one on the table to dispel the darkness. The light shone on the big bed sitting there, reflecting off the dresser's mirror. A large pitcher full of water sat on the dresser, along with some towels and wash clothes. Ann took off her shawl, and stood looking at her reflection in the mirror as she folded it and laid it over the back of a chair. She paced around the room, and Jim knew she was nervous, it was her wedding night. He sat back in the overstuffed chair giving out a contended sigh as Ann perched on the edge of the bed, her hand around a bedpost.

Jim looked at her." Are you nervous Ann?"

"A little," she laughed," I guess."

He laughed with her," I understand."

"Jim, what you said earlier, did you mean it?"

"Yes, all of it Ann."

"I do love you Jim, I have for a long time, but I really did not know until after you had left and I lost you. I have missed you terribly."

"You never lost me Ann", he said softly, "for I thought of you every day an' long lonesome night I spent away from you. I told you before that I always knew I would come back, an' now you are my wife." She got up off the bed and came over to him, sitting in his lap, her arms sliding around his neck. He pulled her to him as their lips met in a long heart pounding kiss. Ann felt the hunger, the needing in his kiss, and she trembled a little, for she had strong feelings herself. She pulled back and looked deep into his eyes.

"Turn out the light," she whispered.

Ann turned back the covers on the bed, and they undressed in the room's darkness. They lay on the bed side by side not talking. As her soft hand found his, he turned to her, kissing her soft warm lips tenderly. He ran his hand down her smooth body, feeling her tremble, her breath coming hard, and fast.

"Be gentle," she whispered in a husky voice.

"I will," he replied, his voice deep and rich with passion.

He positioned himself over her, and slowly he made her a woman. There was a sharp pain, as she cried out softly, but soon the pain was gone, and they consumed their marriage. Now that they had joined, she was his wife, his woman and they were truly husband and wife. After it was over, they lay in each others arms filled with the soft glow of lovemaking. She slept on his arm that night, and the next morning when he reached for her, she came to him willingly and passionately enjoying the feel of his body. At breakfast that morning, Ann found that she was famished and ate heartily as did Jim. He looked across the table at her, a big smile on his face.

"You make a beautiful bride Ann."

She gave him a warm glance, her brown eyes soft and full of love." Thank you husband."

"After eating, we will pick up some supplies at Burkes before we head home. Home. Been a long time since I had one."

"You have one now Jim and I will see to it that it is a happy one." He smiled at her, the love and pride showing on his face. Paying the check, he walked down to the Livery to collect the team and Buggy, after leaving Ann at Burkes to order supplies.

"Howdy Jim," Mose greeted him. "Yuh aire lookin' mighty chipper this mawnin. I believe bein' married agrees with yuh."

Jim laughed, "it does Mose when you are married to the

sweetest, prettiest girl in the country."

Mose agreed with that.

At Mose's call, his grandson brought the team out and hitched them to the Buckboard and Jim paid him for the nights keep, giving him an extra dollar. The young boy grinned and slipped the dollar into the pocket of his faded jeans. Jim drove over to Burkes and tied the team to the hitch rail. Going inside he saw that Ann was stocking up on much needed things at the ranch, including tobacco and rolling papers for the old men at home. He slipped up beside her and put his arm across her shoulder.

"Looks like my wife is buyin' you out Fred."

Fred was all smiles as he waited on Ann." Good tuh see yuh again Jim, an' congratulations tuh the both of yuh."

Jim carried the supplies out and piled them in the back of the buckboard, then going back inside told Fred," add to that order, two hundred rounds for my .44 Colts, two hundred for my .44-40 Henry, an' a hundred rounds for my .50 Sharps."

Fred looked up, a surprised expression on his face."Yuh aimin' tuh start a war Jim?"

"No," Jim said, but I may have to finish one!"

Fred shook his head as he filled the order, glancing at Jim from time to time.

Ann stared at her husband, a question on her lips, but he just Smiled at her. As they drove out of town, the sun had pushed the long shadows away, and was beginning to heat up the land. Entering the wide canyon that opened up into the range, the sun shone on both sides of the canyon walls, making different colors. Browns, purples, blues, dark grays, blacks, and a reddish tint at the bottom of the walls. Ann put her arm through Jim's.

"All these colors, and you can only see them in the morning here." He nodded," yeah, right pretty".

On the ride back to the ranch, they talked of future plans, ways to improve the ranch, and of the new life they would share together. Ann kept her arm linked with his all the way home. When they pulled into the ranch yard, Smoky ambled out of the Blacksmith shop, and waved a cheerful greeting.

"Wal Miss Ann, yuh don't look much different, "cept fer thet new dress," he laughed as he helped her down from the Buckboard seat. She gave him a bright smile, "morning Smoky."

Jesse and Wess came up from the corral smelling of dust, horses and sweat.

"Howdy newlyweds," Jesse called, a big smile on his weathered face. Wess added his well wishes as the young couple stood side by side, Jim with his arm around Ann.

"Well boys, soon as we get these supplies put away, we will have a conflab," Jim said," an' get this situation straightened out around here."

Soon the supplies were put away in the store room to Ann's satisfaction. Smoky put the team up and Buckboard in the barn. Jim had started a fire in the cookstove, and the big coffee pot was boiling. Jim also set out a bottle of whiskey, Ann brought out some glasses and Jim poured drinks for him and the men.

"Heah is to yore good health an' prosperty," Jesse toasted to the couple. The toast was echoed by Wess and Smoky.

After the glasses were empty, Jim sat down and looked at Jesse. "Now, let us do some serious talkin', fill me in on everythin'." For the next two hours they talked cows, range conditions, Sloans, the surrounding countryside and people there. After that Jim had a pretty clear idea of the situation here.

"Now, if you all will clear out, I will start supper," Ann told them. The men went out in the front yard to sat in the shade of some old Cottonwoods. Benches had been built under them years ago and they perched on the rough seats. Jim lit a slim cigar looking out over the range, the rolling hills and grassy plains."

"In the mornin', I am goin' to take a long ride. I know pretty close to where the boundrys are, but I need to refresh my memory. I doubt if it has changed that much."

"Wal, yuh ought tuh know son," Jesse spoke up," yuh rode this range fer several years."

"Yeah, an' even then the Sloans were pushers. Never could get enough land or cattle to suit them. Not very neighborly either."

"Frum what I kin hear, John Sloan is on his deathbed," Jesse said. "He was always a tough, mean tempered man," Jim mused," rough on everybody around him, includin' his own sons."

"Yep, an' thet oldest son uv his, Jack, is jist the same as his pa wuz, maybe worst. Somethin' fer yuh tuh keep in mind Jim, is thet they all hate yuh fer shootin' Mark an' leavin' him a cripple."

"No use to worry over somethin' that happened in the past Jesse. Now, while I am gone, I want you all to stay close to the ranch. Never know when some of them might decide to pay us a visit here".

"One uv us is always hyar with Miss Ann," Smoky told him, but then none uv us stray too fer from the place anymore. They aire some cattle back in them grassy valleys we ain't been able tuh gather up on account uv havin' tuh be gone from the ranch an' leavin' Ann hyar alone". The old man looked worried.

"I aim to put an end to the Sloan's way of doin' one way or another," Jim uttered in a cold icy voice.

The three old men there knew he would too. Jim Rivers was young, fast with a gun, good to his friends, but Hell on his enemies. They also knew that he would straighten the Sloans out, and get them off the Rocking R's back, so they could get back to the business of ranching without looking over their shoulder every time they were out on the range. The Rocking R was on it's last legs when Jim rode in, but now they had hope, putting their future in his hands. Ann came to the door then calling supper, and the talk broke off as they filed in to eat.

After supper Jim and Ann sat on the front porch watching the sunset together. As the sun dipped in the western sky, shadows grew longer and the land took on a rosy tinge, bathed in soft glows. Soon a Whippoorwill began his lonesome call, and upon the hill behind the house, an Owl gave out his mournful cry. Coyotes were in full chorus, their yipping and howling filling the night with their weird sounds. Ann snuggled closer to Jim on the old blanket covered swing, her head on his shoulder.I know they are just Coyotes, but they still give me goose bumps sometimes."

Jim laughed softly in the darkness. "Out on the lone prairie sometimes at night, they were my only company. It is a lonesome sound, but still I felt a kinship with them, for I was lonely myself, but not anymore."

He cupped Ann's face in his big hands and kissed her full red lips. "I could get used to this," she mummered softly.

"Me too," he said.

Soon after they made their way to the bedroom where Ann had always slept since she was a girl. Her mother had died when she was young, and her father and Uncle Jesse had pretty much raised her with the help of a neighbor woman, who taught her the ways of being a young lady with poise and manners. When she was sixteen, the neighbor lady and her husband sold their ranch moving off to California, but by then there were instilled in Ann, the qualities to shape her life, to make her into the woman she was today.

Next morning Jim rolled out early as was his habit. He poked up the fire in the big black cook stove and put on the coffee pot. By the time he had shaved and washed up, Ann came into the kitchen dressed for the day, a smile for him on her face.

"Morning husband."

"Mornin' wife."

She turned up her face for a kiss, and he obliged her, holding her close. By the time the coffee was beginning to boil and the ham and potatoes were sliced, Jesse came in with Smoky and Wess. While Ann made the biscuits, Jesse fried the ham and potatoes in large iron skillets. The good smells in the roomy kitchen brought back memories of other days and other meals here, back when Ann's mother and father were still alive. As the eggs cooked, Ann slid two pans of golden brown biscuits out of the oven. There was a smudge of flour on the tip of her nose, a happy look on her face. They sat at the table, making small talk as they ate. Soon the platters were cleaned and it was time for Jim to leave.

He went into the bedroom and came out packing two heavy rifles. Ann walked down to the corral with him carrying his saddle bags which were full of food and extra shells. She watched as he saddled up his black stallion slidding the rifles into their sheaths. He turned and took the heavy saddle bags from her settling them into place. Ann had a forlorn expression on her face that told of her worry for him. As he turned again, she grabbed him in a fierce hug, holding back her tears. He put his arms around her kissing her soundly, then pulled back to admire her beautiful face. She looked up into the strong face of her husband and felt her heart throb with love for him.

What would she do now if something were to happen to him? No, she must not think like that. She forced a smile, "please be careful Jim."

"I will Ann. Things like this have been my job for years. Being careful an' studyin' out things have saved my life several times. Don't worry about me."

He tipped up her face with gentle fingers and kissed her again." Stay close here till I get back to you Ann."

He swung and stepped into the saddle, tipping his hat to her. Ann watched him until he was out of sight, his tall broad shouldered frame sitting loosely in the saddle. The tears came then, she turned and with dragging feet slowly made her way back to the ranch house. It would really be lonesome here now with Jim gone. She did her usual chores that day, washing dishes, cooking, gathering the eggs, working in the garden, but still the time dragged. Finally night came and now she had to face that empty bed, the one she shared with Jim. It was late when sleep at last claimed her.

CHAPTER 6

As Jim rode along, what Jesse had told him ran through his mind. "Wal, a few cows missin' hyar an' thar. A steer butchered out once in a while. Pot shots took at us when we wuz out on the range. Cattle drove tuh different places, water holes plugged up. Small things like thet. Kept us jumpin' frum place tuh place all the time. None uv us wuz ever hit by a bullet, but thar wuz some close shaves. One time a rifle bullet hit the horn uv my saddle. Thet hoss had a fit. Took off like his tail wuz on fire. Couldna' been nobody but thet Sloan bunch, cause they aire the only ones tuh gain if we give up. Few little ranches 'round hyar, but they ain't never give us any trouble. Most uv them aire friendly folks. Now, thet Jack Sloan has jist aboot pestered Ann tuh death tryin' tuh git her tuh sell out tuh him, but she never would give in. Then he wanted her tuh marry him. Maybe she didn't give him a earfull over thet. He jist wanted this ranch. Got so she could hardly go tuh town without him apesterin' her. Finally one day in Burkes store she told him off good an' proper, an' after thet, things got worse. I am tellin' yuh Jim, thet girl was at her wits end till she thought of you, an' I sent yuh thet telegram. Ever since yuh come back hyar, I hev seen her perk up an' be like her old self again. She loves yuh son, believes in yuh. Them years yuh wuz gone, she talked about yuh a lot. Never got over thinkin' she had wronged yuh. Other fellars hev tryed tuh make a place in her life, but she would have nothin' tuh do with 'em. Said yuh would be back some day an' she would be waitin fer yuh."

Jim's blood got hot and a mean tempered feeling stole over him as he thought about Jesse's story. Well the Sloan's time would come. Jim remembered Jack Sloan as a tall man about his size, dark hair, mean dark eyes, and a Mexican mustache. Hard on horses and men. Wore his bone handled gun tied down low in a cross draw. In Arizona during the 1870's guns were the law when Judge Colt was holding trial. "Remember son Jesse had told him, thet bunch hates yuh like the Devil hates holy water, an' they aire the kind thet will shoot yuh in the back an' think nothin' about it"

At the Box S ranch house, three men sat around the kitchen table.So, now thet little filly has hitched up with Rivers, I 'spect he will be on oure trail sooner er later," spoke the man with the black mustache.

"Yep, spliced up tight," the thin man with the white scar on his left cheek replied. "We gonna hev tuh take care uv Jim Rivers Jack."

"In time Snap, in good time. Thet Sheriff ain't no fool an' if Rivers gits shot too soon, he might start lookin' at us a whole lot closer then he has in the past."

Changes things some don't it Jack?"

"Yeah Bill, it does at thet. We gonna hev tuh be real kereful how we handle this. Let's jist give it some time an' maybe things will change oure way."

A wheel chair came rolling into the room, a man in it , his shrunken, useless legs covered with a blanket; "Jack, Pa seem's worse."

"Worse how Mark?"

"He is talkin' out uv his head, callin' fer Ma tuh bring him a drink uv water."

Jack stood up," Bill, go fer Doc Weaver."

His brother Bill got up without a word and hurried out the

door. A few minutes later there was a clatter of hoofs as he headed for town. Jack and Snap went into the old man's bedroom with Mark wheeling along behind. John Sloan, head of the clan lay feverish and rambling in the big four poster bed he had shared with his wife for many years. The Mexican woman tending him rung out a clean white cloth in a pan of cool water and laid it on his hot sweaty brow. His breathing was labored and irregular, almost at the point of panting.

"Is thet yuh Nancy," he called hoarsely, in a quavering voice?

"Yes, it is me," the woman answered in a soft voice, "rest now." She looked up at Jack and Mark shaking her head. They stood or sat around the silent bedroom that was already shadowed with death, no one talking, all watching the man's labored breathing. They knew he was dying, that it was only a matter of time. The ticking of the clock on the mantle was loud in the quiet room as it ticked away the last minutes of his life. Soon the Doctor came rushing into the room with his black bag and checked the old man over. John Sloan muttered incoherently, the slurred words making no sense to the people who heard them.

Suddenly he sat upright in the bed crying out,"Git away frum me Damm yuh," then fell back. The men who were seated there stood up quickly, all eyes riveted on him as he lay back. John Sloan gave out a loud groan, as his life left him in a long hissing breath. Doc Weaver checked for a pulse, and after a minute closed the wide staring eyes. He sighed as he looked at the brothers gathered there and shook his head."I am sorry boys, he is gone," he said as he put his stethascope in his black bag.

"We will hitch up the wagon an' bring him intuh town," Jack told him as he stared at the body of his dead father."

Doc Weaver nodded," I will wait and ride in with you."

Within the hour the men were headed for Rimrock and the funeral parlor there. Jack and Bill rode on each side of the wagon, and Mark rode in the buggy with Doc Weaver, his wheelchair piled in the back.

Jim continued on his journey over the Rocking B range. He found several head of cattle, but they were scattered all over. He made a quick count as he checked the water holes and grazing areas. This range could hold twice the cattle on it without over grazing at all.

He had a sudden thought, what if instead of driving the cattle off and selling them, they had just driven them into some of the long deep valleys in the hills. There was hiding places for several hundred head without crowding them. As he rode, he thought of the day he had arrived back at the Rocking B Ranch after recieving the telegram.

He was having a look around the ranch. The Rocking B brand was burned into the barn, shed doors and all the buildings were in good shape as was the corral. There were several fine horses in it. All the Smith shop tools hung on the wall, an Anvil and Forge stood in the center of it. A few saddles and bridles hung on pegs there. Smoky, Jesse and Wess hung around waiting for orders of some type. After his tour of the ranch buildings, Jim had turned to the men.

"Smoky, you and' Wess stay around the ranch today. Me an' Jesse are goin' to have a look around."

Jim noticed as he and Jesse rode out, that Smoky sat on a bench in front of the bunkhouse, while Wess was down by the barn. Both wore six guns and carried rifles.

"Yuh proably know this range as well as me Jim, yuh
rode over it 'nuff times when yuh worked hyar fer Dave."
"I remember it Jess."
"Anythin' in particular yuh want tuh see?"
"No, just ride around."

The sun was low when they rode back in. Smoky and Wess strolled over as they unsaddled their horses, and turned them into the corral.

"See anythin' out uv the way," Smoky asked as he rolled a smoke?" Nothin' out of the ordinary, just lookin' around," Jim had answered. 'What stock we seen looked fat an' slick. If Sloan had this ranch, he would control the grazin' an' water for miles."

"Thet wuz oure way uv thinkin too," Jesse had put in.

"Ann knew all this when she sent for me, didn't she."

Jesse had nodded his grizzled head at that.

"Well, I will see to it that she don't lose one cow, or a foot of her range!"

The three old hands had looked at each other and grinned. Suddenly they felt young again. Laughing, they made their way to the house and into the kitchen.

"I hope you boys are hungry," Ann said as they marched into the kitchen.

Seemed they all were.

She had loaded their plates with beefsteak, beans and fried potatoes. That along with hot biscuits and hot coffee made a meal for a hungry man. After supper the three old hands headed for the bunk house for a few hands of cards before bedtime. Jim sat at the table with Ann over another cup of coffee. He pulled out a long slim cigar lighting it at the top of the lamp chimney, and blew out a stream of blue smoke."Ann, I began to see what you are up again here."

"Yes. The last year after Dad died has been rough on all of us."

"You should have sent for me after Dave died."

"I did not know where to get in touch with you Jim."

"I was movin' around a lot then."

"I wonder how the Sloans will take your coming back."

He had shrugged his broad shoulders," I really don't care one way or the other Ann."

"I am sure when they hear of it, there will be trouble."

"We will take it one day at a time. An' don't forget, tomorrow is our weddin' day Ann."

And now she was his wife and he owned half of the Rocking B Ranch with her as his partner. Let the Sloans do what they dared, he would handle them one way or another.

As Jim rode across the range, three riders a few miles from him were sitting their horses looking at a bunch of Rocking B cattle, Shad Walker had pointed out.

"Thar is a nice little bunch uv cows," He told the other two. "We culd drift over thar, cut out a few head an' drive 'em over tuh Sycamore Crossin'. Make us some drinkin' money."

"Wal now Shad, Jack said tuh leave them cows alone, cause he plans on gittin' 'em all at one time," Cork Blair said.

"Hell fire Cork, he ain't gonna miss twelve er fifteen head."

The offer hung there in the air as they looked at each other.

"I don't know," Cork replied as he shook his head.

"Whut about yuh Slim," Shad asked?

"Wal now, I would not mind tuh hev a few dollars in my pocket, an' a bottle. Sides, Jack ain't hyar now nohow."

"All right then, what aire we watin' fer," Shad grinned, showing yellowish teeth.

Gigging their horses, they crossed over deeper into Rocking B land and in the direction of the cattle. Above the cattle, a rider sat his mount in the shade of some tall pines. He had a pair of strong binoculars looking the country over when he saw the riders approaching toward the cattle. Freezing on the spot he made out three riders cutting out a small bunch." Ah, rustlers."

Turning his horse, he headed in a direction that would intercept them, and riding swiftly he made for an out cropping of rocks a mile or so away. Getting there well ahead of the rustlers, he ground hitched the big black and pulled both rifles out of their sheaths. There was a giant Pin Oak that shaded the rocks, and he knelt down under it. He laid the two rifles down and put a sack of cartridges on a flat rock beside them. Sliding back the breech lock of the big .50, he slid a shell into its chamber.

The slow moving herd of bawling cattle were moving closer to where he was hidden. As luck would have it, they were going to pass right in front of him. He relaxed and watched as they got closer and closer to his position. Jim knew the cattle were Rocking B because he had read the brands through his glasses. He grinned to himself. The rustlers would be in for a big surprise. When they were within range, Jim bellowed out, "HANDS UP RUSTLERS!" His shout pealed down off the rocks like the voice of doom. Caught in the act, the rustlers stopped and sat their saddles staring up at the rocky cliff.

"We ain't rustlers," one called back," we aire jist pore cowboys doin' oure job!"

One of them, a man in a black and red checked shirt slid his rifle from under his saddle and took two quick shots at the place in the rocks where the voice seemed to come from. Jim sighted in the Sharps on him just as a bullet ricocheted off a gray boulder by his shoulder showering him with dust and chips. "BOOM"! The big .50 roared and the man in the checked shirt was knocked backwards out of his saddle to lie crumpled on the ground. The echo of the Sharps bounced off the rocks sounding like a cannon in the still air. "BOOM"! The Sharps bellowed again and Cork Blair's horse reared and fell backwards, rolling over on it's rider. The big .50 spat again, the .240

grain bullet plowing up dirt and grass in front of the third horse. It bucked and pitched throwing Shad Walker to the ground with a hard thud.

Jim blew down the barrel of the Sharps to help cool it off, and laid it on the rocks beside him. Picking up his binoculars he surveyed the scene below him. In less than a minute, one dead and the other two on the ground. The man whose horse had thrown him slowly got up staggering around. The other one whose horse had rolled over on him was sitting up and it looked like he had a broken leg. Jim sheathed his guns and mounting his stallion rode down there. He sat in his saddle, right hand near his Colt. Looking them over he told the man standing there staring at him;

"Seems like you boys bit off more that you could chew."

"I know yuh, " the man sitting on the ground with the broken leg spat out,"Yuh aire Jim Rivers."

"I know you too Blair. Rustler, wanna be badman, half ass gunman."

Cork Blair stared hard at Jim, "Yuh killed my pard Slim!"

Jim looked at him out of icy gray eyes. "Just be glad it wasn't you Blair. You was on Rockin' B range drivin' off Rockin' B cattle an' that makes you a rustler in my book."

"Now jist a minute," Shad blustered," we wuz only pushin' 'em back on thar own range."

"Looks like to me you was pushin' them toward Sycamore Crossin'," Jim retorted with a wintery smile.

"Whut yuh gonna do with us," Cork wanted to know?

"Ought to hang you, but I recon I will take you into town an' turn you over to the Sheriff."

Jim could see the relief on their faces when he said that.

"I need help gittin' on a hoss," Cork Blair said.

Jim nodded at Shad. "Help him, but first bring your gun an' his over here to me!"

Shad hastened to obey, and when he had Cork mounted, pointed to Slim.

"Whut about Slim thar?"

"Load him up across his saddle an' take him with you."

After much grunting, pushing and lifting, Shad finally got the limp body across the saddle and tied down. He turned to Jim with sweat rolling down his face, his breath coming in long gasps. "Yuh aire a hard man Rivers!

"Now," Jim ordered," bring me Slim's pistol an' all the rifles here an' if you feel lucky just go right ahead."

Shad shook his head, gathered up all the guns carrying them over to Jim, who put the pistols in his saddle bags, and tying the rifles together with piggin string, hung them on the side of his saddle.

CHAPTER 7

As the little calvacade made it's way toward Rimrock, Jim sat with his thoughts on the way to town. What were these three doing rustling Rocking B cattle, and a small bunch at that? Maybe they were just picking up a bonus, some drinking and gambling money. Maybe Jack Sloan thought he had the ranch sewed up and the hands were helping their-selves to some easy money. Well, now that he had started the fight, let the chips fall where they may. He was not one to back up when he got started. Didn't matter what he had to do, Ann and the Rocking B would be protected. Riding down the main street, he drew several stares, but rode on till he got to the Sheriff's office. Tom came out the door as he dismounted.

"Howdy Jim."

"Tom. Got some customers for you. One needs a doctor an' the other needs the undertaker."

"Umm. So I see." He raised the head of the dead man, then let it drop. "Slim Waters. Might hev knowed thet. Them three always ride together."

A small crowd had gathered around, talking and gesturing. Tom looked over at them.

"One uv yuh go fer Doc Weaver an' tell him tuh come over tuh the jail, an' another uv yuh go git the undertaker."

"Whut aire the charges Jim?"

"Rustlin' an' attemped murder Tom."

"Ah huh. Help yore friend tuh a cell Walker, he looks kinda pale 'round the gills."

Cork groaned and cussed as he was helped into the jail.

Doc Weaver came out of the cell and poured himself a cup of coffee from the ever ready coffee pot. Taking a sip, he sat down in a chair looking up at the Sheriff. "Well, I have set Blair's leg and splinted it up and bandaged his ribs. That is about all I can do for him at this time. He will proably hollar some time to time. If he gets to hollaring too loud, give him two of these pills Tom."

"I will Doc, thanks."

Doc Weaver picked up his black bag and left.

Tom Blaine settled back in his wooden swivel chair and looked across his desk at Jim. "Now, tell me what happened."

So Jim told Tom his story from start to finish. Tom leaned back in his chair puffing on a cigar as he listened, his eyes appraising the young man across from him.

"Wal, I guess now it has started. Have any plans?"

"Yeah I plan on hiring two or three hands an' rounding up a small herd an' driving them to the railhead as soon as I can. We could use the money. Course I have saved most all I made over the years, but that will be my ace in the hole."

Tom nodded sagely." I see. So yuh think thet if the Sloans aire goin' tuh pull anythin', they will wait till yuh git the herd gathered before they hit."

"That is my thinking. Anything can happen during a stampede."

"Yeah, like it happened to my friend Dave."

Jim nodded in agreement.

Tom settled deeper in his chair." Thar is one Sloan yuh will not hev tuh worry aboot."

"Who is that?"

"John Sloan, the old bull of the herd. He died yestiddy an' they aire buryin' him in the mawnin'. All the crew an' the boys aire grievin' down at the Red Horse."

There was a glint in his eye as he said it.

Jim shook his head, "I have to get back out on the range anyway."

He stood to leave, and Tom raised up out of his chair to shake his hand. It was a firm handshake between old friends.

"Luck Jim."

"Thanks Tom."

Jim camped that night in a wooded hollow where a small spring furnished him and his horse enough water for their needs. He put the stallion on a long picket rope so he could graze on the thick grass. Building a hat sized fire, he sat his little coffee pot on a flat rock beside it to heat. Digging into his saddle bags, he brought out a slab of bacon and a dented skillet. Slicing off the bacon he lay it in the pan balanced on some rocks. While it was frying, he opened a can of beans with his Bowie knife. Soon the tantalizing smell of frying bacon and boiling coffee filled his nostrils.

Darkness fell as he was eating his meager meal. Hoot Owls called from the timbered ridge and night birds fluttered around as he sat there in the darkness sipping another cup of hot coffee, relaxing, smoking a slim cigar. How many lonely camps like this had he seen over the years. Now though, he was content. Thoughts of his lovely wife Ann filled his mind. After all those lonesome years moving around from town to town and job to job he had a wife and a ranch. That to defend them both he would have to use his guns, that much he knew and was ready for any challenge. The Rocking B contained over fourty thousand acres all told, including grazing land, gullies, rocky plateaus, waste land and timbered lands. A big land. A land where a man could grow and raise a family. A land a strong men could tame, make something of himself.

Dave Belton along with John Sloan had come into this part of Arizona about the same time, only Dave had gotten here first and claimed this range. Sloan carved out his ranch next to it. They had been friends then, but over the years John Sloan had cast envious eyes at the lush grass lands and waters that Dave Belton controlled. After that things begin to happen. Little things. It all came to a head one day when Dave caught Bill and Jack Sloan driving off a small herd of his cattle. He threw a gun on them, relieved them of theirs and took them to their father with their hands tied behind them, slumped in the saddle.

Harsh words were spoken that day. Words that could not be taken back. John Sloan was boiling mad. Mad at his two sons because they had been caught, and mad at Dave Belton because he had caught them. Dave had laid down the law that day and Sloan had to take it, because Dave Belton was fast with a gun plus he had Jesse and Smoky to back his play. So John Sloan stood on his porch and swallowed it, his yellowish brown eyes burning with hate for the man before him. He never forgot that day carrying his hate with him to the grave. Now both Dave and John were gone, but Sloan had passed his hate down to his sons and Jim knew as sure as the sun rose in the East, that there would be trouble with them, and soon.

He thought of Ann again as he sat there, remembering her warm, soft body close to his as they lay in bed. Sighing, he got up, checked his horse, giving him a friendly pat, then he unrolled his bedding on a soft spot, taking off hat, boots, and guns, stretched out on it, pulled a blanket over him and was asleep. A sliver of moon peeked over the far hills casting a soft, feeble light on the man lying there.

Jim awoke in the gray dawn, kindled a small fire and put on the coffee pot. As the coffee boiled, he saddled Midnight making ready to ride out. From what he remembered, he was close to the Rocking B's boundary on the south side of the ranch. If he rode in a rough circle, he would cover most of the outlaying land of the ranch. He wanted to take a look in the canyons and deep valleys back in here. The sun was showing it's face at him as he rode at a smooth trot. Keeping a wary eye peeled, he stopped often taking long looks at the land through the binoculars, sweeping from side to side. Far off he caught sight of riders and knew he was close to Sloan's land.

He stayed off the ridges and hills keeping to the low places so he wouldn't be skylined, staying in the trees and deep shadows as he moved along. Walking his horse up a long draw leading to a canyon, he heard bawling cattle. Drawing his Colt, Jim eased his way toward the sound. At the end of the draw was a rough pole fence and gate. The walls of the canyon serving as a ready-made corral. Dismounting, he swung the gate open on it's rawhide hinges and leading Midnight, he walked deeper into the canyon. It covered at least a hundred acres covered with knee high grass. A small stream ran down one side of it. There were cattle scattered all over the floor of it. Mounting, he rode forward at a walk. Stopping in what seemed to be the middle, he sat his saddle studying about what he had found. Making a rough count, he figured there were over two hundred fifty head of cows here. He rode through them finding Rocking B among the herd, and counted four different brands all together. There appeared to be no one around.

Evidently the cattle had been here a while for the grass was eaten down short in places. Getting around them, he started them moving toward the gate and out onto the range. They had been penned for some purpose, but what? Proably for someone to pick up later. Drive off several small bunches, move the others around and no one would notice right off. But Who? The Sloans? Who else could it be but them. Jesse had told him there had been no trouble with any of the small ranchers in the area. Maybe there were other missing cattle penned up in other canyons. From what Jesse told him, they were missing around a thousand head. From what he saw today, around two hundred of the cattle he had found were part of the missing thousand. So that left eight hundred head unaccounted for. They were hidden here somewhere, he could feel it. Sloan was smart enough to know that if he drove stolen cattle to market, no matter where, someone would see and tell of them. No. Jim grinned at the nerve of the cattle thieves. Steal cattle and hide them on the same range they had been stolen from. That way no one would see the cattle and by discouraging riders from looking by shooting and threats, there was little chance of them being found.

After he got them moving along, he turned Midnight and headed back into the foothills. Whoever hid this herd must have others hid out. It made sense to him now. Sloan was playing a deep game, but now he was not dealing with old men or small ranchers with no one but themselves to depend on for help. That was part of Sloan's plan. Bleed Rocking B dry a little at a time. Keep them from making a drive, steal off the cattle bit by bit and hide them out, then when the Rocking B was broke with all it's cattle gone, step in with a big hearted offer and buy it up for nickles on the dollar. That made it clear to Jim. As Sloan had been siphoning off the cattle, he had the gall to ask Ann to marry him. She only had the three old men to help her now, and Jesse and the others pulled the rest of the herd in close to the ranch where they could be watched better. Of course a sweeping raid by a bunch of armed men could take the cattle, but Jim did not think Jack Sloan wanted any attention drawn to him in any form. And now that Jim was back and married to Ann, he would have to be really careful of anything he pulled. Why would Jack Sloan not want attention focused on him? Was there another iron in his fire? Jim needed to talk to Tom Blaine about his suspicions and thoughts.

  He would have to be on his guard day and night. A frosty smile touched his face. Before dark he found three hundred head penned up like the others, in a long deep almost hidden canyon. Jim knew that Jesse and the other two would never leave Ann alone long enough to search out all the canyons and hidden valleys on the Rocking B. After getting them headed back in the right direction, he made camp for the night, and after a megar meal, rolled up in his blankets. He had no fear of anyone sneaking up on him with Midnight on watch. By the time the long shadows were rolling up for the day, he was well out on the trail. Riding up a small draw he heard cows bawling like they were being pushed. Leaving his horse ground haltered he climbed the hill beside him and knelt beneath some fragrant Cedar trees with his glasses. He saw the cattle then, moving along slowly, being pushed by four men. He took it to be about three hundred head. Jim could read the brand on them, Rocking B. Slipping back to his horse he drew the 44.40 Henry from it's sheath and made his way back up the hill. Another thought came to him. They could steal the cattle, keep moving them around on this vast range and no one would ever be the wiser. They would not have to hide them all. A cold smile touched his lips, just cowboys doing their jobs! He let the men get nearer until they were in close rifle range then he called out, "HANDS UP RUSTLERS ", his voice pealing out across the space between them! The men drug iron, shooting at the voice. Jim emptied the Henry into them. Horses bucked and snorted, dust flew, rustlers hit the ground, cattle bawled and milled around stirring up more dust. Jim did not shoot to kill, but to try and turn the herd. They were turning, bellowing and snorting in their panic. All was bedlam and confusion. Reloading he dusted them again. The two men who were thrown from their horses finally got back in the saddle again. There was no more shooting from any of them now as they turned their panic stricken mounts and hightailed it away in a new cloud of dust, the maddened cattle right behind them. Jim sent a few more shots after them to help hurry them along. Soon they were out of sight and the cattle had slowed down somewhat, heading back into the lush grass they had been driven off of. That Jack Sloan is really a arrogant Bastard Jim thought as he reloaded the Henry.

Mounting up he rode back out of the boulder strewn void onto the grassy range land following a small stream until he came to a gushing spring and there he made camp for the night. Digging out a couple of hard biscuits and some jerky, he made do with that and some hot coffee, all the while thinking about one of Ann's good hot meals. After eating he cleaned all his guns and oiled them, checking the actions. Later he lay in his blanket gazing up at the stars so far above him, white and gleaming, hands behind his head thinking. The moon was high when he finally drifted off to sleep.

CHAPTER 8

Jack Sloan stood in the Sheriff's office staring over the desk at him, a deep scowl on his face.

"Whut in the Hell do yuh mean rustlers Tom," he shouted?

"I mean they wuz caught tryin' tuh run off cows frum the Rockin'B range," Tom shot back," thet is whut I mean by rustlers. They shot at Jim Rivers, an' he shot back at 'em. Killed Waters an' shot Blair's hoss from under him!"

"They wuz not rustlin, they wuz jist drivin' 'em back on their own range cause they drifted!"

"Never the less, they aire gonna stand trial fer it," Tom answered cooly.

Sloan fumed and snorted."Whut about Rivers?"

"Rivers wuz defendin' his life an' his property."

"Why the Hell aire yuh takin' up fer Rivers Tom?"

"I ain't takin' up fer Rivers, but, he could hev killed all three uv them an' been within his rights as a property owner."

"By Gawd, yuh ain't gittin' away with this Blaine," Sloan hissed!

Tom Blaine stood up to face Jack Sloan eyeball to eyeball. "Aire yuh threatenin' me Sloan?"

"No, I am not threatenin' yuh, but I do not like it at all, leaves me short handed."

Tom Blaine gave him a cold stare from gray, icy eyes.

"Well, what about bail fer my men?"

"No bail. Thar will be a hearin' next week when Judge Barkley gits back. He will hev the final say. "Till then, they stay put!"

Sloan gave him a hard look, spun on his heel and stomped out, slamming the door behind him. A smile creased the Sheriff's face. Let him stew on that for a while. Just then his deputy, Harm Stevens came in.

"I jist passed Jack Sloan on the sidewalk, an' he looked like a thunder cloud," he announced.

"He is used tuh gittin' his own way, an' this time he didn't," Tom said.

Harm nodded as he rolled a smoke. "He shore likes tuh be the tall hog at the trough, don't he."

Tom shook his head." Harm, watch over things till I git back."

"O K Sheriff," Harm told him as he sat in a chair by the desk.

Tom pulled a Winchester 44-40 out of the gun rack and stepped out onto the board walk. Turning, he headed off in the direction of the livery stable.

As the Sheriff was leaving Rimrock, Jim Rivers was cutting across the range on his way back to the Rocking B and Ann. He rode out of a coulee onto the flatland, home on his mind. As he rode past a grove of small oaks, he saw a flash of light reflecting off metal. He spurred Midnight and slid over the side of the running horse. A bullet kicked up dirt under the flying hooves of the stallion as Jim headed for a pile of rocks to his right. When he got there, he pulled Midnight to a sliding stop, and grabbing his Henry from the saddle boot, he dived behind the rocks. At his command Midnight galloped off out of danger.

Lying in the safety of the circle of rocks, he peered out and a bullet cut a white streak across the rock near his head. He was within easy rifle range, but so were they. The trees were not real close together and he began to make out shapes among them. Putting his hat on the ground beside him, he eased the long barrel of his Henry over a flat rock and took aim. At the shot, there was a startled yelp and he knew his shot had been close.

There were several shots coming his way, searching fire meant to flush him out. He laughed. No dice boys. I have fought Indians before. Try a new trick. Peering closer, he made out a shape lighter than the bark of the oaks. He lined his sights up on it, took a long breath, let half of it out and squeezed the trigger. The Henry roared and he saw the man stand up straight and then fall sideways.

It was hot lying there in the rocks and he wished for the canteen on his saddle, but to move meant certain death, so he lay like a lizard, only his eyes moving. Over in the oaks the three men there were getting impatient.

"Damm yuh Bart yuh shot too quick, "Snap Wilson complained in a low voice.

"I thought I had him dead center," retorted Bart," he must hev eyes like a hawk."

"He shore ain't no pilgrim," Bat Smith remarked," never wuz."

"Lets load up an' pepper thet rock pile good an' hot," Snap told them.

Bart looked over at his friend on the ground, a bloody bullet hole in his chest." Bored him plum center," he mumbled to himself.

"Ready," Snap asked?

All three men shot as one, the bullets knocking chips off the rocks around Jim. He lay as flat as he could on the hot ground as the chips and dust fell all over him. One sliver hit his cheek drawing blood. Lucky there were no rocks much behind him for the bullets to ricochet off of. Jim never moved or fired a shot. Let them think they had killed him. Maybe then they would rush him. Then the tables would be turned on them.

Suddenly there were more shots, but from a different direction. The rifle fire from the trees stopped. He risked a look. The ambushers were running for their horses and he helped them along with a few shots, but they rode away keeping the grove of trees between them, him and whoever fired the other shots. Warily he got to his feet, wiping at the blood on his cheek. A man with a raised rifle rode out of a slight draw and came forward leading a big black horse that Jim reconized as Midnight. He stood watching as the man got closer then saw that it was Tom Blaine. He grinned as Tom got closer.

"Good to see you old timer."

"I wuz ridin' out tuh the Rockin' B tuh see yuh when I heerd the shots. Found yore hoss in thet dip over thar an' figured the shots had somethin' tuh do with yuh Jim."

"As far as I could tell, there was four of them hid in that oak thicket an' they started shootin' at me. I managed to drop one of 'em though."

"Let's go over an' check on him then."

Jim mounted Midnight and they rode over to the small grove of trees, rifles at the ready. As they drew nearer without any body shooting at them, they began to relax. Jim swung down as Tom kept his rifle trained on the woods and walked cautiously toward where he saw the man fall. He lay there in the leaves, his lifeless eyes staring at the sky, his face set in the throes of death, a bloody stain on the front of his shirt.

"Come on in Tom," he called over his shoulder.

Tom came through the leaves and sticks till he came to where Jim stood. He looked down at the dead man and gave out a deep sigh." Bob Long, one uv Sloan's riders."

Jim looked at Tom." Yesterday afternoon before sundown, I saw a herd of cattle being driven by four men. One of them wore a black hat with silver discs on the head band, now, there lays the hat! I shot into them to scare 'em off, an' now I believe they got around in front of me after they figgured out who I was trying to cut me off from the ranch an' drygulch me. Seemed like you changed their plans for them Tom."

"Glad I wuz passin' by son."

Jim found the man's horse and led it back through the trees.

"Yuh might as well keep them guns uv his Jim, he won't be needin' 'em no more whar he is."

"Yeah I will put them with the others I have collected."

They laid the dead man over his saddle tying him in place. Then leading his horse out past the trees, gave him a slap on the rump and watched him gallop off the direction of the Box S.

"No need fer them tuh know I had a hand in the fight today," Tom said, "cause I want tuh play dumb as long as I kin on this deal. I will ride back tuh the ranch with yuh Jim."

"Glad for the company Tom. Sloan seems to have it in for me all right."

"Wal, yuh married Ann an' now own half uv the Rockin' B an' he wants it bad."

"He will shore have Hell gettin' it."

"I know the Sloan bunch had a hand in Dave bein' killed, an' he wuz my good friend. Never could git no evidence on 'em though. One uv these days I will ketch 'em at somethin'." He looked over at Jim," I am shore glad tuh see yuh back."

"I would have come home sooner Tom if I had known Dave was dead an' Ann bein' hard pressed like she was, I shore would have."

"She wuz proud son, wanted tuh make it on her own. Jesse tryed, but he is like me, gittin' old. This is a young man's game. Now, thet man we sent home over his saddle will raise questions. None uv the others seen who I wuz. Now maybe that ain't the way a Sheriff should play the game, but I want 'em tuh make a mistake, a big mistake so I kin raise a posse an' bring 'em in."

"The only way most of them will come in is tied over their saddles. What makes a man like Sloan do the things he does Tom?"

"Greed, hate, envy. Thar is a empty place in them that cain't ever be filled. They want more an' more. Thar is never enough. John Sloan swallered up every little rancher he could. Maybe nothing illeagle, but he preyed on thar weakness. Over the years he got tuh thinkin' he wuz above the law. Now he is layin' in the graveyard, an' all thet schemin' fer land, he wound up with with a six by three foot piece uv it. Them boys uv his will end up the same way".

The ranch came into view as they rode along talking. As they neared the house, the door flew open and Ann came running out to leap into Jim's arms. Tom stood there, a big smile on his weathered face. Jim helt Ann close kissing her and being kissed in return. When he sat her down on her feet, there was a rosy tint on her lovely face. She had a sweet smile on her face.

"I bet you two are starved," she said, holding on to Jim's hand.

"I am," Jim laughed.

"Wal Ann " Tom told her," yore cookin' is always welcome."

"Where are the men," Jim asked?

"Out with the herd, something has been bothering Uncle Jesse the last two days and they have been staying out late. They won't be in till well after dark."

"Wal Jesse is mighty savy about things. If he feels somethin' is oot uv place, it usally is," Tom said, giving Jim a deep look.

Ann brought them hot coffee, and they sat there talking as she fixed ham and eggs. She put in a few words about what Jesse had told her, but it wasn't much help. After they ate, Jim and Tom walked outside and down to the barn leading their horses. Tom puffed on his old black pipe as Jim unsaddled Midnight and rubbed him down. He peered through the smoke at the young man before him.

"Reason I rode out hyar tuh see yuh Jim wuz tuh ask a favor."

"Go ahead Tom."

"Things around hyar aire rougher then most people know. In the last couple years, Jack Sloan has been bringin' in some hired guns. Snap Wilson is one, Shad Walker is another. Then thar is thet Smith boy thet calls hisself the Sundown Kid, who you met fust off when yuh come back. Walker an' Smith aire suspected uv bank robbery an' murder up in Colorado. No proof again them thet kin be found. Also a stage holdup in Utah. Wilson has been a paid gunman in two er three range wars. Hell on wheels with a gun, but also a backshooter. Durnin' them range wars, several men wuz shot down frum ambush an' he wuz suspected. Again no proof. I am jist one man here Jim, an' can only do so much as Sheriff. You can see whut I am up again".

"When Jesse told me thet yuh wuz comin' home, I sent word tuh a friend uv mine. A captain in the Arizona Rangers. He is deeply interested in them two an' a few more up oure way. Wanted tuh send a Ranger up hyar tuh look into it, but I told him I had a idee thet might work better. Told him I knew a man who fit the job I hev in mind."

He stopped and puffed at his pipe, a twinkle in his eyes.

Jim stared at his old friend as what he had just told him sank in

"Kin yuh guess what I am gittin' at Jim?"

"I think so Tom, you want me to take the job." It was a flat statement.

"Will yuh do it son? I know yuh hev worn the badge before cause I hev kept up with yuh ovar the years."

"How do we work it Tom?"

"I hev the papers an' badge in my wallet an' I kin swear yuh in right now. Only catch is, yuh caint tell nobody, not even Ann."

Jim nodded his acceptance.

There in the shadow of the barn, Tom swore him into the Ranger service. Jim hid the badge and papers in an inside pocket of his vest as Tom looked proudly at him.

"Thar has been rumors of a small group of men holding up stage coaches an' rustlin' cattle all around this part of Arizona. Nuthin is ever touched around hyar close. All uv these things happen a hundred miles er more away. They reach up into New Mexico an' Colorado. The rangers feel because uv thet, they aire based hyar close. Sort of keeping their own doorstep clean."

"You think Jack Sloan and his gun hands are doin' the robbin' Tom?"

"It is beginnin' tuh look thet way. Men fittin Bill Sloan an' Snap Wilsons decriptshun hev been seen at some uv the holdups. I smell a rat around hyar Jim. I think Jack Sloan is the head uv thet gang thet is doin' the stealin', an' then posin' as a honest rancher 'round hyar. He has too much money fer a rancher an' is free handed with it. Big time gambler. Always hangin' 'round town spendin' money."

"It shore is something to think about," Jim agreed.

CHAPTER 9

The horse carrying it's dead rider came walking into the Box S ranch yard it's head hanging, reins trailing the ground. Mark Sloan was sitting on the porch in his wheelchair watching as the horse limped in heading for the barn. There he stopped and snickered, blowing tiredly. An old puncher came out of the barn to see what the trouble was. When he saw the dead man tied across the saddle, he gave out a loud shout. Three men came out of the bunk house, looked came came running toward the barn.

"Hell Fire," one exclaimed," its Bob Long!"

"Didn't he leave with Bill an' Snap," another asked?

"Yeah he did," spoke up the other man, " he shore did!"

The old hand came up to the porch where Mark sat watching.

"Who is it Lem?"

"Bob Long," Lem replied, gazing at Mark through watery eyes.

"Bob! Thet makes two dead an' one uv oure hands shot up since Rivers come back. Damm his hide!" he exploded, beating his fists on the arms of his prison. He stuck both arms up into the air. "If only I could walk!," he cryed out," if only."

The day after, Bill and Mark sat with Jack in the office of Kirby White settling the estate of their father. Kirby peered over his wire rimmed glasses at them.

"John left all his worldly goods to you boys. Ranch, cattle, money in the bank, ect."

The brothers nodded. They knew they would inherit everything, but their father's will had to be probated through the courts. Judge Owen Barkley sat off to one side, a fat cigar in the side of his mouth.

"Now, if you will sign here Jack, seeing as how you are the executor, that will wind up everything."

Jack dipped a pen into ink signing the doucument.

"The deed to the ranch is free and clear," Judge Barkley said," so that is it. You boys have inherited a large ranch plus several thousand head of cattle. Which if you manage it right, should keep you comfortable for many long years."

"Pa never liked owin' nobody nuthin," Jack remarked, "He wuz a self made man."

"Yes he was," the Judge agreed.

Standing, Jack and Bill nodded to the judge and lawyer then strode outside with Mark following in his wheel chair. Outside Jack stared down toward the jail, a thoughtful expression on his face.

"We got tuh git Shad an' Cork out uv thar," Bill said, reading Jack's thoughts.

Jack rubbed his chin . "We will when the time is right. A old Sheriff an' one Deputy won't be thet much trouble."

"Whut about Rivers," Bill asked?

"This ain't none uv Rivers put in, but if he pokes his nose intuh it, so much the better."

"I don't know Jack, seems pretty risky breakin' them out."

"Hell fire Bill, we aire fifteen tuh thar three."

"We wuz fifteen Jack. Now we aire thirteen an' thet is a unlucky number."

Jack looked at his brother and snorted." Losin' yore nerve Bill?"

"It ain't thet Jack an' yuh know it, but I got a funny feelin' about me frum time tuh time here lately."

"Whut kind uv funny feeling?"

"I don't really know. We usted tuh jist ranch, maybe run off a few head uv cattle every once in a while fer drinkin' an' gamblin' money. But these things we aire mixed up in with Snap an' Shad an' Sundown, wal, it sorta bothers me some."

"Look Bill, none uv the jobs we pull off aire around hyar close," Jack hissed." Nobody kin lay anythin' at oure door. This trouble with Rivers is a old grudge thet everybody knows about. They ain't stickin' thar noses into it. Proably Blaine will nose around a bit, but he caint do much about things thet happen out on the range miles away frum town. Quit worryin'. We make plenty out uv them quick raids. Hell, most uv them aire pulled off a hundred miles away from hyar. We kept it frum Pa an' we kin keep it frum the the rest uv the people around hyar."

"Yeah, all right Jack, but what about Shad an' Cork? If they stay in thar an' go tuh trial they jist might talk, to try an' make it easier on tharselfs."

"I hev thought about thet Bill an' thet is why we got tuh come up with a plan tuh git 'em out seein' as how the Judge denied bail. Fer now let's jist git back tuh the ranch."

They loaded Mark in the back of the light spring wagon, tied his chair in place and left Rimrock.

The killing of Bob Long had been on Jack's mind all day and when they got back to the ranch he jumped the Sundown Kid.

"Where the hell is Snap an' the others he bellowed?"

The kid shrugged his good shoulder. "He left with Bob, Matt an' Bart yestiddy mawning. Said they had somethin' tuh do. Bob's hoss brought him in, but they ain't got back yit. Thet's all I know."

Just then there was a clatter of hooves and the three missing men rode in on lathered horses up to the bunkhouse. Jack came out all fired up.

"Whar the Hell yuh been Snap?"

"Workin' some cattle," Snap replied calmly rolling a smoke.

"Whut cattle?"

"A small herd uv Rockin' B stuff."

"Whut the Hell fer?"

"We been doin' it fer some time. A few here an' there, pennin' 'em up."

"Not any more we ain't. We got bigger fish tuh fry now!"

"Like whut fer instance?"

"Like thirty thousand dollars in cash thets whut," Jack told him in a low voice.

Snap whistled,"whooee! When?"

"Come up to the house an' bring Matt an' Sundown."

Jack and Bill headed for the house pushing Mark in his chair followed by the other three. Inside they sat at the kitchen table as Jack brought out glasses and a bottle of whiskey. He looked over at Snap.

"Now tell me how Bob got killed."

Snap told him from when the rifleman had opened fire, and up untill Bob had gotten shot;" We laid a trap fer Rivers, but Bart shot too soon an' missed him. When thet other rifle opened up, we skedaddled out uv thar. Figgured Rivers would bury Bob."

"He sent him home over his saddle. We buried him this mornin."

Snap made a motion with his hands. "I hate 'cause Bob got plugged, but them bullets wuz flyin' 'round us like bees an' we didnt hev time tuh take him with us."

Jack waved away his half hearted apology." Lets make plans."

As usual Mark sat on the edge of things. He nursed his whiskey and silently cursed Jim Rivers for his useless legs.

Jack spoke in a low voice." The payroll fer the Swift Minin' Company is comin' in by stage friday. Them miners ain't been paid in a month an' the payroll comin' in is fer this month an' next. Thar will be two guards in the stage plus the shotgun guard on top. Jist three men tuh guard all thet money." He showed them an evil smile.

"How many men we takin', Snap asked?

"I figgure me, Bill, yuh, Sundown, Matt, Bat, an' Shad. Seven uv us ought tuh git the job done."

"But Shad is in jail."

"Not fer long. I mean tuh break him out, him an' Cork."

"Cork won't be no use tuh us with a broke laig Jack."

"No. But if I leave him in jail he might talk if he gits mad. We will git him out an' hide him some whars in one uv the line shacks."

"How do yuh plan on gittin them out," Matt wanted to know.

"I figgered it all out on the way home," Jack told him.

Two days later, a young boy on a lathered pony rode up to the Sheriff's office, flung himself out of the saddle and ran into the room all excited.

"Sherriff yuh got tuh come quick. Thar's been a bad shootin'!"

Tom Blaine stood up." Hold on thar son, slow down. Now tell me whut has happened tuh git yuh all worked up."

"A man has been killed Sheriff!"

"Who son?"

"That settler that lives over on the edge uv Rockin' B, Will Martin!"

"How do yuh know he has been shot?"

"I met a friend uv his on the way tuh town an' he asked me tuh ride in an' tell yuh so he could ride back tuh Martin's place!"

"Yuh shore about this son?"

"Yessir Sheriff. He even give me this dollar to come fetch yuh." He extended a trembling hand with a silver dollar in it.

"All right son. Git on back home now an' I will ride out thar."

The boy ran out the door, jumped on his pony and dug out.

Tom got his rifle from the gun rack and hollared for Harm.

"Harm, I got tuh ride out to the Martin place. Seems like somebody shot him, maybe killed him."

"Go on Sheriff, I kin hold things down hyar."

Tom walked down to the livery stable, got his gray horse and rode out of town. Something about the whole thing didn't make sense to him. It was over twenty miles out to Martin's place, so Tom nudged his gray into a fast lope as four pairs of eyes watched him leave town. As soon as he was out of sight, they rode in towards the jail slowly, spread out so as not to attract attention to theirselfs. The four men walked their horses up an alley to the back of the jail. There were two extra horses with them for the men inside. They dismounted, pulled up bandannas to cover their faces and while one stayed with the horses, the other three drew their guns, and going up the side of the jail, peered around the corner looking up and down the street carefully. They had chosen noon so that most of the people would be eating dinner and off the street. Swiftly the masked men slipped through the front door and into the jail. Harm was sitting at the Sheriff's desk looking through some wanted posters when the door opened and he was looking down the barrels of three big black guns. One of the men motioned him to be quiet, while another took his gun. They tied and gagged him, laying him on the floor behind the desk. Grabbing the ring of keys off it's hook they quickly unlocked the cell door to let the prisoners out. The leader of the trio pulled down his mask. Shad and Cork grinned. They took their guns from the rack leaving the cell, Cork making good time for a man on crutches with one of his friends helping him along and onto his horse. As soon as they were mounted, the six men rode out of town keeping to the willows along the creek bank.

By the time the riders reached the old line camp cabin, Cork was weaving in the saddle. Sweat ran down his face in streams and there was a gray pallor about him. The men got him out of the saddle and into the cabin, lying him in a bunk of tangled blankets.

"Whisky," he croaked.

A bottle and glasses was produced and after a large gulp the pallor left his face, the raw whiskey giving it a ruddy glow. He lay back on the unmade bed as a deep sigh escaped him, dropping off into a dead sleep. Jack Sloan looked over at Bart Short.

"Bart, I am gonna leave yuh hyar with Cork to watch over him. Thar is plenty uv grub an' coffee hyar fer yuh an' yore job is tuh take cair uv him 'till he kin shift fer hisself."

Bart nodded, not too pleased with being a nursemaid, but orders were orders. He stood in the door watching them as they rode off through the Cedars. Picking up a bucket, he walked over to the spring beside the cabin and filled it with the cold clear water. Coming back he built a fire in the small cook stove placing the battered coffee pot on it. As the water boiled, he sat in the doorway smoking as Cork snored and muttered in his sleep.

After drinking a cup of the dark scalding coffee, Bart got the axe off the wall going outside out to chop some wood. He was a good hand with an axe and the chips flew. After filling the woodbox, he went down to the corral and fed the two horses there. By now the day was far gone and he was hungry. He stoked up the fire in the stove, sliced up some ham and potatoes for frying then checked on Cork who was still sleeping soundly. He sat the coffee pot on the back of the stove and dug out a loaf of bread from the rough built cupboard, it's crust as hard as a rock. First thing tomorrow, I am gonna set some sourdough fer buscuits he thought as he filled a plate with ham and potatoes. Bart was a man who liked hot biscuits. He lit a lamp and sat in the feeble glow of it as he ate supper and listened to Cork snore.

When Tom Blaine rode into Will Martin's place, the first thing he saw was Will splitting wood.

"Yuh swing thet axe pretty good fer a dead man Will." he said by way of greeting.

Will looked up, "dead man, whut aire yuh talkin' about Tom?"

So Tom filled him in on what the young boy had told him. Will took off his hat and ran his fingers through his still dark hair.

"Ain't been no body 'round hyar fer close tuh a month Tom. Somebody must have been pullin' yore laig."

Tom sat in his saddle, a puzzled look on his face, his brow knitted in thought. "Yeah. Well, it got me oot uv town anyway."

"Maybe somebody wanted yuh out uv town fer some reason Tom."

"An' I believe I know why too," Tom growled.

"Git down an' set a while Tom an' I will git my wife tuh fix us some coffee."

"Thanks Will, but if my hunch is right I better git back tuh town pronto, soon as I water my hoss."

After watering his gray and checking the saddle chinch, Tom mounted and headed back to Rimrock in a cloud of dust leaving Will staring after him.

About the time the Sheriff was leaving Will Martin's ranch, a group of dark garbed riders mounted on powerful horses were riding north to intercept the stage carrying the Swift mining payroll in the edge of Colorado. The Swift Mining Company had mines in lower Colorado and upper New Mexico. Seven heavily armed men rode to relieve them of their money. A swift holdup, take the money and hightail it back home. A simple plan that had worked for them several times in the past.

CHAPTER 10

Jim and the ranch hands drifted the Rocking B cattle in closer to the ranch. There was plenty of good grazing and water there for them and they could be watched easier. A small creek flowed down from the foothills and the grass was tall and rich there.

"Whut is on yore mind Jim," Jesse asked?

"I been thinkin', there are proably more of our cattle still back in the hills I ain't found yet."

"Humm, could be at thet son."

"Tomorrow I will take a long ride back through where I did not get a chance to go before, look around, talk to some of the other ranchers back in there."

"Take yuh a week tuh do thet Jim."

"Maybe not. There ain't many places where cattle could be hid without a lot of hard work."

Jesse rolled a smoke as he sat in his saddle, a thoughtful expression on his leather brown face. "Pretty slick uv Sloan. Drive off a small bunch at a time an' hide 'em instead uv sellin' 'em. Make us think rustlers wuz stealin' us blind an' keep us broke. Tom asked 'round, but nobody wuz buyin' cattle with a Rockin' B brand er one thet had been altered. Made us both began tuh wonder."

"Sloan wanted to bleed the ranch dry, scoop it up for his own price, then rebrand the cattle he had stolen, drive them back on the ranch an' after the brands had healed, say he had bought them in New Mexico or down in South Arizona.

"A good plan," Jesse admitted, an' it wuz headin' that a way son, but Sloan is in the clear. Them two hands in jail aire all thet can tie him to it, thet is if they will talk, but they will proably swear they done it on their own hook. Say whut yuh will about Jack Sloan, but he takes care of his men."

"He is shrewd, no doubt about that," Jim agreed, "but somewhere along the line he will slip up."

They circled the herd, helping Smoky and Wess settle them down.

As they sat over supper that night they were discussing winter feed.

"If I remember right, there are some high pastures the cattle never get to that would make tons of hay," Jim said.

"Thets right son," Jesse spoke up, "only lately we been too short handed tuh cut it an' stack in thar."

"That barn loft will hold a lot of it an' the rest could be stacked close, if we had somebody to cut an' haul it down here."

"I got a idee," Smoky spoke up, Will Martin has a small ranch back in the foothills an' three sons. They might be willin' tuh cut thet hay a stack it Jim."

"That is a good idea," Ann chimed in. "Will used to work for us before he settled on his own place, and his wife is a friend of mine too."

"All the small ranchers need cash money," Jim mused, "I will see Martin in the next day or two an' put the deal to him.
"Are you riding out again Jim?Yes Ann, I am goin' to check the other canyons an' places I missed before.""How long will you be gone?"

I figgure three days or more. I am going to see the other ranchers an' ask if they have been bothered with rustlers."

She got up from the table and started cleaning up the supper dishes. The three old hands said their goodnights shuffling off to the bunkhouse.

"Here, let me give you a hand," Jim said picking up a dishrag. You wash an' I will dry."

"If your friends could only see you now," she laughed, giving him a peck on the cheek.

He grinned with happiness. "I am a changed man wife."

Ann felt her heart swell with pride and love for this tall man beside her. She had loved him for years knowing he had loved her too. After the dishes were washed and put away, they went out to sit on the porch watching the sunset. Big billowing, gray and white clouds rode on the rose and blue ones below them. Shades of purple, pink and black blended in their colors as the sun slowly slipped away. Twilight lingered, then faded away to darkness as almost timidly, a few faint stars showed their faces. Somewhere out on the prairie a coyote's lonesome call sounded and a horse down in the corral snickered at something, stamping his feet.

"I guess we better get to bed Ann if I am goin' to get up early in the mornin'"

"Yes," she answered, moving closer to him, offering up her soft lips for his kiss.

Their lips met and it seemed like a sweet fire shot through their veins. Rising, they went inside, closing the door behind them making for the bedroom. They undressed in the semi darkness, crawling into bed where they lay holding each other tight. Their lips met as their arms went around each other.

"Oh Jim, I missed you so much when you were gone, "she whispered softly in his ear.

"I missed you too Ann," he mummered as he slowly lowered his body to hers.

They came together and were joined as one. Their lovemaking was slow and sensual as they soared on the wings of Angels, slowly coming back to earth, seeming to float on air. Their passion saited, they fell asleep in each others arms.

Early next morning Jim slipped out of bed trying not to wake Ann, but she felt him leave her side and sat up, a smile on her rosy face, her long hair tousled and awray, a blanket helt up to her bare breasts.

"I tryed not to wake you." he said.

"While you are getting your things together, I wil fix you some breakfast."

He smiled as she slid out of bed, her naked body white in the predawn light. She slipped into her pants and a blouse, tying her streaming hair back with a red ribbon. She followed him into the kitchen and while he got the fire going, fixed the coffee pot. He went out then to saddle Midnight. When he came back, the coffee was ready and breakfast almost done. He poured a cup of the hot liquid and sat at the table watching her deft movements. Their eyes met and he smiled, remembering last night, the feel of her soft, smooth skin, the hot passion they had shared.

All too soon Jim was gone before the other hands came in for breakfast. After they left, she started the housework, counting the hours until Jim returned to her. About midmorning she heard a horse coming up to the house. Picking up the pistol she kept close to hand, she went to the door. With a sigh of relief she saw that it was Sheriff Blaine. Opening the door, Ann walked out on the porch to greet him.

"Morning Tom."

"Mornin' Ann," he called back.

Tying his horse he came through the yard gate, up the steps and onto the porch.

"How about a hot cup of coffee Tom."

"Sounds good."

He followed her into the neat kitchen and took a chair, lying his dusty hat on the floor beside him. He sighed and looked up.

"Jim hyar Ann?"

"No, he rode out at daylight this morning. Said he would be gone three days or so."

"Whar did he go?"

"Said he was going to check and see if any more of our cattle were penned up in the back country. He was planning to meet with some of the small ranchers back in there."

He nodded thoughtfully as he sipped his coffee.

"Did you need to see him Tom?"

"Wal, somethin' happened in town that will intrest him."

She sat down beside him. "What happened?"

"Them two rustlers he brung in was sprung yestiddy by three masked hombres."

"Oh, I see," she exclaimed!

"They tied Harm up an' broke 'em oot in broad daylight. Got clean away without bein' seem at all."

"Where were you Tom?"

"Wal thet has been a naggin' at me. A young boy come runnin' intuh my office hollarin' thet Will Martin had been shot, maybe killed. Said a man stopped him out on the range an' told him to fetch me out thar. Even give the boy a dollar fer doin' it. Said he had tuh git back out tuh Martins. When I rode out thar, Will was bustin' wood. I see now thet it wuz a setup tuh git me out uv town. They wuz proably watchin me all the time."

He drained his cup and stood to leave. "Tell Jim when he gits back. An' don't worry Ann, yuh got a man thet will bust this range wide open."

Ann stood watching Tom ride away, her hands at her breast, worry over Jim finding a place in her mind.

Late on the next afternoon after he had left the ranch, Jim rode into Will Martin's yard. Will stood on the porch, rifle in hand watching him ride up.

Jim waved a hand, "howdy Will."

Martin looked closer at the tall rider, then a big grin split his face.

"Wal I'll be dammed, if it ain't Jim Rivers! Git down friend an' let me shake thet good right hand!"

Jim climbed stiffly out of his saddle and shook Will's out stretched hand warmly.

"Damm it Jim, I am glad tuh see yuh. I thought it wuz you when I seen yuh ride up."

Will's wife Barb came out of the house to stand by her husband. She smiled at Jim," good to see you again Jim."

He took off his hat and smiled back at her. "You too Barb. How you been?"

"Wal, we been hearin' a lot about you Jim," Will told him.

"Like what Will?'

"Fer one thing, thet yuh hev declared war on rustlers 'round hyar."

"And that you married that cute little Ann Belton for another," Barb laughed.

Jim grinned sheepishly at them. "Yeah, we got married."

"I told Will all along that all you needed was a good woman to keep you in line. I am proud for the both of you Jim. She needs you."

She poked her husband in the ribs. "If Will hadn't married me, no telling what kind of trouble he would have got into on his own."

Will laughed. "She is right Jim. We settled this place, course it ain't much, but we run two hundred head uv cows, put in a few crops an' I got three sons tuh help me."

"I have a job in mind I want to talk over with you Will."

"Whut kind uv a job Jim?"

"Work for you an' your boys, if you want it. Pays cash money."

Will stood thoughtfully, nodding his head as he looked at Jim.

"Why don't you talk it over after supper, it's ready and on the table," Barb said.

As Will and Jim were washing up, the three boys came in from their chores. They spoke to Jim looking his guns over carefully as they washed up. Jim ate heartily of the Venison and fresh vegetables on the loaded table. After supper they sat on the porch smoking as Barb cleaned up the table. The boys sat on the edge of the porch watching and listening.

"How old are your boys Will," Jim asked?

"Abe is sixteen, George is fourteen an' Joe is twelve.

"They look like workers to me Will."

The boys grinned and glanced at each other. Barb came out and took a seat by Will, wiping her hands on the apron she wore.

"They are good workers Jim."

"That job I mentioned is cuttin' hay for the Rockin' B Will."

Will laughed," thet is one job we know about."

The boys agreed, and looked eager at the prospect of work.

"There is a mowing machine an' a couple of wagons at the ranch. If we can get together on the price, the job is yours."

"How much hay we talkin'?

"Near as I kin figgure, between fifty and sixty acres."

"Right smart bunch uv hay."

"Yeah, it lays in three different platues above the ranch, an' like I say, the job pays cash money."

Will looked around at his wife and then at the boys; "Wal, thar ain't no doubt we could use some cash money Jim. What about hosses?

"We have horses for you Will an' we need the hay for winter."

In a few minutes they had agreed on a price and shook hands on it. Jim walked down to the barn to check on Midnight before he turned in. He slept in the Martin's hayloft that night in the sweet smelling hay dreaming of Ann.

After taking breakfast with the Martins next morning, Jim made ready to ride. He talked to Will as he saddled His horse.

"Have you seen any movement of cattle around here Will?"

"Whut kind uv movement Jim?"

"Like maybe they did not want anybody to see them. Maybe hid out cattle."

As Will studied on that, his wife came down to the barn bringing Jim a small bag of food to take with him.

"Come tuh think on it, Abe wuz huntin' back over toward Black Oak Canyon, an' said he thought he heerd cows bawlin' back in them canyons. He did not go to see though, cause thet canyon is a good place tuh git lost er hurt in."

"Black Oak Canyon. I remember that place Will. Used to hunt horses back in there."

"Ride soft Jim."

Barb handed him the food." You tell Ann I am coming to visit her when Will and the boys come to cut hay."

Even though Barb was twelve years older than Ann, they had always been close friends. Her husband was two years older than her.

"She will be tickled to see you Barb."

Jim rode away with a wave of his hand. Black Oak Canyon. If memory served him right, there was a hanging valley back in there. He rode with his Henry across the bow of his saddle, eyes and ears alert for any sound or sudden movement. Midday found him entering the gloomy valley, it's towering walls and dark, deeply timbered hills cast a foreboding pall over the country side. The craggy cliffs rose straight up, looming stark and forbidding. There was a almost erie quietness back in here that set a man's nerves on edge. A lone Eagle sailed high overhead, floating on the currents of the air, barely moving his wings. Midnight's hoofs sounded loud on the rock floor and he saw tracks of both cattle and horses in the dust almost lost to sight. So, cattle had been driven through here.

He followed the dim trail under the canyon walls, listening close for any sound of cattle. The big canyon split near the back going in two separate ways. The tracks he was following stayed to the right hand side and as he rode along, noted that he was gradually climbing. The trail wound around the hill through timber and rocks until he came to the top. Just below the crest was a grass filled valley with a small creek running through it. The hanging valley he had heard of, and there in the lush grass was a herd of cattle. Cut trees choked the entrance blocking the cattle from climbing out and forming a crude gate. He sat his mount looking the valley over. Pulling his binoculars out of his saddlebags, he took a long look at the cattle there. The ones he saw wore the Rocking B brand. He figgured the valley at over a hundred fifty acres. There seemed to be over two hundred head here." Well I am onto your tricks now Jack Sloan. Soon I will have proof on you too. Might as well leave 'em here for the time being', what do you think Midnight?" The stallion flicked his ears, pawing the ground as Jim talked to him. Turning his horse, he rode out of that lonesome, desolate place and started across the prairie.

CHAPTER 11

In the three days he had been gone Jim had made a long circle without finding any more cattle hidden out. In fact he believed he had found what was left of them and felt no need to search anymore. As he rode into the ranchyard, tired, saddle sore, hungry and sweat stained, he saw that Will and his boys had already begun the haying. Will's place was only five or six miles away as the crow flies so it was easy for him to drive back and forth every day. In the days when Jim rode for the Rocking B two ranch hands did the haying. Ann was waiting for him at the yard gate with a smile and a kiss.

"Ah Jim, you smell like horse and sweat."

"I know. I am going to soak in that tub of yours a while, then shave these whiskers off. After that, I will be ready for company."

In behind the kitchen Ann's father had built a small room with a big tin tub in it so they could take a hot bath. Water for it was heated on the stove and poured in. The only drawback was that the water had to be emptied by hand also. At the same time he had put in a hand pump in the kitchen so they wouldn't have to carry water from the well. There was water heating on the stove when they went in. Jim placed his saddle bags in the bedroom with a tired sigh. Smoky had taken Midnight down to the barn for him.

"Hot water," Jim exclaimed! "How did you know I would be back tonight Ann?"

"I didn't, but I have to take a bath too you know."

"With me," he laughed?

"If you like," she replied blushing.

"I would like," he told her.

He filled the tub, Ann locked the doors and they stripped and stepped into the roomy tub, where they spent a long hour, soaking, laughing, talking, and making love.

At supper that night, Jim told them what he had done and where he had been. Ann told him what Tom Blaine had told her the morning he had left. Jim did not seem too surprised at the news. Jesse plied him with questions as Wess and Smoky listened intently. Ann broke up the talk when she sat two spicy dried apple pies on the table. After two slices apiece, the men gave up. The older men bade them goodnight leaving Jim and Ann at the table.

"You know Jim, those masked men who broke the other two out of jail must have been pretty daring doing it in broad daylight."

"Yeah, or afraid the other men would talk."

"You think that was the reason?"

"I do. Jack Sloan is high handed in all things. They rode for him according to what Tom told me. He had to have been behind the breakout."

"Do you think they are hidden out at his ranch?"

"It would be like looking for a needle in a haystack Ann. Tomorrow I will ride in an' have a talk with Tom."

They lay in bed that night, Ann with her head on his shoulder, talking about the future plans for the ranch.

"We could plant one of them big creek bottoms in Alfalfa so we could have plenty of feed for the cattle in the winter. That along with the upland hay would support a good sized herd."

"We would need money Jim."

"I told you before not to worry about money when I came here Ann."

"Why, are you rich Jim?"

"No but I have a few thousand dollars in a bank in Flagstaff"

She sat up and stared at him. "What?"

"I saved nearly all my money I have made over the years Ann. The last drive I made to Dodge City, I was partners in it with an old rancher who needed to get his cattle to market. Said it was his last herd 'cause he was getting out of the business of buyin' an' sellin' cattle. His trail boss had got hisself shot in a saloon fight an' he needed a man quick. I was in town, an' somebody told him about me, so he hunted me up an' offered me a good deal. I took him up on it. I made good money on that drive, an' I put it in the bank with the rest of my savin's. The way I lived, I did not need much money.

As Ann listened, she could hear the loneliness in his voice. What had he been through the five years he was away? What had he suffered being alone? Her heart melted for him.

"What about kids Ann? Do you want children?"

"Yes I do. What about you?"

"I shore do. A couple of boys to help me run the ranch, an' a girl for you."

"I think four would be a nice number Jim."

He chuckled. "I guess all women like babies."

"This one does," she said, snuggling closer to him.

The snuggling turned into kissing and the kissing turned into something else as they threw their clothes on the floor.

At breakfast next morning Ann asked Wess to hitch up the buckboard.

"I need to do some shopping," she told Jim.

"Be glad for your company Ann."

They drove out, the wheels on the black shiny buckboard stirring up as much dust as the horses hoofs. Ann looked at the fat cattle grazing peacefully on the lush grass along the shining creek that ran the length of the Rocking B. The swaying flowers and the green willows along the banks.

"It is a beautiful land," She exclaimed. "A strong land. A land to grow with. My father's sweat and blood are in this land and my mother's toil and gentle ways. Now they are gone Jim and it belongs to us. To work, guard, and preserve for our family to come."

"Yes," Jim agreed, "it is all that an' more. My mother an' father are buried in the Rimrock cemetery near yours. Both of us was born here, grew up here, went to school together an' now we are grown up an' married. I grew up in my father's Blacksmith shop learning about iron an' how to use it, dreamin' about bein' a cowboy. After he died an' the shop was sold, your father gave me a job here on this very ranch we own now. My roots are here an' I want to live out my life here on this land with you Ann an' our family."

She gripped his strong arm for she felt the same as he.

In town Jim left her at Fred Burkes store while he went across the street to the Sheriff's office. Tom sat behind his desk sorting papers as Jim entered. He looked up and grinned.

"Jim, come in son, hev a seat."

He dropped down in a chair across from the Sheriff.

"Ann told me about the jailbreak Tom, can't say that I am surprised at all."

"No dammit. Thet story about Martin throwed me off."

"Got any ideas?"

"Yeah, I got a idee, but as usual, no proof."

"Sloan seems to be gettin' bolder as time goes on."

Tom nodded his gray head, "one day Jim!" His mouth closed like a steel trap.

Jim filled him in on what he had been doing, and about finding more of the stolen cattle. Tom listened attentively, nodding from time to time.

"Jack Sloan is damm slick Jim, but one day he will slip up."

Ann was through with her shopping when Jim came back. She gave him a big smile. "I am ready to go if you are."

"How about eatin' dinner before we leave."

"Sounds good to me. Shopping always makes me hungry."

"Hey Fred, we will pick up these things when we come back,' Jim called.

Fred waved a friendly hand.

In the hotel dining room, Jim admired his lovely wife. She had bloomed out in the last few weeks. Her face was rosy and her eyes shone with new life. His coming back had made a lot of difference in her he thought as he remembered her that first day. She drew looks from every man in there when they entered. He was proud to call her his wife. They took their time over lunch and lingered over coffee and pie. There seemed to be so much they needed to say. Finally, they stood to leave with Jim holding her arm as they walked back to the store.

As they were driving home, she turned to him. "Jim, when can we make a drive?"

"Soon as I can get some hands."

"I know you told me you had money in the bank at Flagstaff, but I feel I need to do my part. That was money you saved while you were gone. I feel that it belongs to you alone."

Jim laughed. "The day we got married Ann, half that money became yours, just like half of this ranch became mine. I wanted to come back as a man of means, not a broke fiddle foot drifter."

"I do not care about the money Jim, it is you I want. Just you!"

He put his arm around her. "We ain't broke honey, so just quit worrying."

"Oh you darling you," she laughed as she lay her head again his shoulder.

The stage coach robbery had gone off as planned. Jack, Bill and the others rode into the ranch yard one night, their saddle bags bulging with loot. They had surprised the guards and the holdup was done without a shot being fired. As the others unsaddled and took care of the horses, Jack and Bill hid the money. This was the third big job they had pulled.

Hidden under the floor of the tack room was an old safe. It had been put there by their father who said he did not trust banks or bankers. Jack unlocked it and put the money inside. Outside he told the men part of it would be divided up later.

"Yuh don't want tuh be flashin' a big roll uv cash 'round too soon after a robbery. If we aire careful an' keep takin' it slow, they won't never catch up with us. The man who passes me the information on shipments is scoutin' round now fer another haul." He looked up at the pale sky. "Daylight will soon be here, let's turn in."

The next few weeks passed by peacefully. Jim hired the Martins and another young man called Bud Johns to help out with the cattle. The boys took to cowboying as if they were born in the saddle. They recovered all the stolen Rocking B cattle driving them back onto their own range. The Martins had the first cutting of hay in the loft stacked for the coming winters feed, and Will came over whenever Jim needed another rider.

Over at the Box S, Jack Sloan planned their next raid.

Ann was happy being a new wife and her love for Jim deepened as the days passed. She enjoyed fixing his favorite meals and deserts. Now that there were more hands to cook for, Jim had hired an old camp cook to fix the meals for the rest of the crew. Jesse, Wess and Smoky were delighted with the new arrangnents. He and Ann took long rides out on the range, but the Sloans were always in the back of his mind. He knew they hated him, that one day the range would be rocked by gunfire. Tom informed him of the stage holdup, but nothing came of it, so they watched and waited. The stealing of cattle had stopped, but it could just be the quiet before the storm. A couple of new hardcases with the look of guns for hire written all over them had turned up in Rimrock.

One day as they were sitting on a hill under the shade of a giant Oak, Ann looked over at Jim and asked; "Do you think Jack Sloan has given upon on our ranch?"

He watched the grazing cattle for a long minute. "No, I do not. He is just bidding his time waitin' for a openin'. He hates me so bad for killin' his friend an' puttin' his brother in a wheel chair that he will never forget, or forgive. His hate is eatin' at him an' in his own time he will brace me. As for now, I think he is up to somethin' else."

They sat in silence for a while looking out over the grassy plains, and enjoying the light breeze whispering through the grass.

"Jim," Ann asked suddenly, "you never had a girlfriend all the time you were gone?" She looked deeply into his eyes as she spoke, reading the expression on his face.

"Never had time for one. Like I told you before, I was always too busy staying alive for girls. Did you ever have a boyfriend?"

"No. I always had you on my mind. Oh, I went to parties and dances where boys my age were, but, no, no one special."

Jim reached over and took her hand. "It was always you for me Ann."

"I feel the same as you Jim."

They sat side by side, holding hands, not talking, just enjoying the closeness of the moment. For the first time in years Jim felt he had accomplished something with his life, something good and lasting. He finally broke the silence.

"We better be gettin' back. I want to get the boys started on that new corral an' shed."

Jim planned to buy some more horses to add to the remuda. When they made a drive, they would need more horses. At the ranch he helped Abe and Bud measure off the places for the posts, driving stakes in the ground.

"Your Pa and brothers will be over tomorrow to help you an' Bud," Jim told Abe.

"Pa is pretty handy with tools," Abe remarked.

"I know son. Your Pa is handy all around."

Abe laughed at that. He had heard some stories about his Pa when he was a young man.

As the sun was rising next morning, Will, his wife and other two boys came driving over in their wagon. George had been staying at the ranch with Abe, but his Pa had needed him a couple of days at home.

"I thought I would come over and visit with Ann," Barb called, climbing down out of the wagon.

Just then Ann came out of the house and down their way, running to Barb, giving her a big hug. They went back toward the house, both talking at the same time.

Jim showed Will what he wanted done leaving him and the boys to their work. Being as how the weather had been dry, he decided to ride out and check Rock Springs. He rode along, alert for any sign of movement, or anything out of the way. The sun felt good on his back, with a slight breeze coming in from the west. When he got there the spring seemed as always, unchecked in it's flow. Four different springs ran out of the giant cracked rock shelf that gave the spring it's name. Sitting his saddle in the shade of an overhanging rock, he heard the sound of galloping horses and backed Midnight deeper into the shadows. A band of dark garbed riders on dark horses rode out of a ravine disappearing into the pines and cedars growing there, heading north. He laid a warning hand on Midnight, "quiet boy." They disappeared out of sight, a bit of dust hanging on the air the only sign of their passing.

"Well now, that was strange, but on the other hand maybe not so strange at that."

He thought it over as he rode back home. Best go into town and have a talk with Tom tomorrow. He had rode over to where the riders came out of the ravine and studied the tracks in the dust. One of the horses had a built up shoe on it's right front hoof. He had seen that track somewhere before and it nagged at him as he rode along. By the time he had unsaddled his horse, rubbed him down and fed him, it was dark. Ann had kept supper in the warming oven over the stove and as he washed up, set it on the table.

"Have you had supper yet," he asked?

"No, I wanted to wait for you". She put her arms around him and gave him a kiss.

"I like kissin' you honey, but right now I am a starving man," he laughed.

She poked him in the ribs. "Sit down then my dear and we will eat. The kissing will just have to wait."

He ate with the hearty appetite of a man of the outdoors. As they ate, they talked of the cattle drive to come.

"We will drive in the early fall when they are fat and slick," he told her.

"How long do you think the drive will take?"

"Upwards of three weeks there an' back to Trails End, the closest shipping place."

"Three whole weeks without you?"

"Maybe less. If we push hard an' don't run into any trouble, could be two and a half weeks."

"A long time to be apart darling."

"Well, how would you like to come along?"

"Me, on a cattle drive? How many cattle are you taking?"

"Me an' Jesse decided on three hundred head. Get them to market quicker, an' give us enough money to tide us over for a while. I want to cull the herd, keep back most of the young breedin' stock. By doin' that, in two years we can make a large drive."

"You really want me to go?"

"Why not. Will an' his three boys are goin' an' so is Bud an' Smoky. You could be our camp cook," he laughed.

"All right, I will take you up on it," she told him.

"You have a couple months to think about it."

"I think it would be a learning experience at that."

"We will see."

CHAPTER 12

Cork was up and around now, helping Bart with the chores around the cabin, but they were both getting cabin fever.

"Why don't you go intuh town an' git us a couple bottles Bart, I will pay."

"Jack told us tuh stay hyar till he give us the all clear."

"Yeah, but Jack ain't stuck in this damm cabin day an' night!"

"I don't know Cork."

Cork wanted whiskey, he needed it, had to have it! The more he thought about it, the dryer he got. For the next two or three days when Bart was asleep, or gone hunting, Cork practiced saddling his horse, mounting and dismounting slowly. It was hard work but he managed it. One morning Bart told him he would gone most of the day. He was going back in the brakes after some fresh deer meat. Cork saw his chance. He would ride into town keeping to the back streets and alleys, come in behind the saloon, get his whiskey, be back before Bart returned.

He gave Bart a good half hour start, then hobbled down to the corral. At his call, his horse came up to him, nibbling at the lump of brown sugar in Cork's hand. As swiftly as possible he saddled up and started to Rimrock. It would be dangerous, but usually at this time of day nobody was in the saloon but the bartender and maybe the old man who did the swamping. Still, he would have to be careful.

As he approached town, he licked his dry lips as his guts cryed out for whiskey. Sweat ran down his face as he walked his horse through the last alley before coming up to the back of the saloon. Already he could taste that whiskey going down as he rubbed the back of his hand across his mouth. At last he was at the rear of the saloon, looking all around him. Carefully sliding out of his saddle, he hobbled slowly up to the rear door. Opening it a crack, he peered inside. The bartender was polishing glasses and the old man was sweeping off the sidewalk. He eased the door open enough to slip through. Being able to use only one crutch helped.

Cork called out in a low voice, "hey," the bartender turned and saw him standing there.

"Bring me four bottles of redeye," Cork told him, "and make it quick."

Sitting the four bottles on the counter in front of Cork, he stepped back. Cork laid some money on the bar, and put another dollar beside it.

"You ain't seen me, got it, he whispered hoarsely?"

"Yeah, I got it," the bartender answered as he picked up the money.

Cork was only able to carry two bottles at a time. He put the first two in his saddle bags then returned for the other two. The bartender handed them out the door for him to grab. Cork could stand it no longer. Pulling the cork out of one of the bottles, he gulped down a big swallow. It burned a path all the way down to his belly, easing the gnawing pain inside. Time to go! As he was sliding the bottle into the other side of the saddle bag, a cold voice stopped him.

"Hold On Thar!"

Cork froze in place.

"Turn around slowly," the voice commanded.

Cork knew that voice feeling the hot blood gush through his veins. He grew mad. Mad at his broken leg, mad at Bart, and mad at the man behind him. His anger caused him to make a bad mistake. Still holding the bottle, he turned his left side to the man in the alley, his right hand grasping his Colt. He turned quickly as he could, a mad curse on his lips, toward the man behind him. His pistol came up, his nostrils flaring, his eyes red with rage at being caught like a kid with his hand in the cookie jar. The other man had a gun in his hand, as Cork's gun came level, the big .45 Colt in the man's hand roared and bucked, flame and hot lead belching out of the long barell!

Something hot hit Cork in the chest like a blow from a sledge hammer. His gun suddenly got too heavy to hold, he pulled the trigger, the bullet kicking up dust in front of the hated man before him, the man with the big Colt. His pistol fell from his hand. He half turned trying to turn the bottle of the whiskey up to his lips. His fingers fumbled and the bottle slipped free and fell to the ground shattering into pieces. Cork fell to his knees. "No," he cryed. trying to reach for it, but instead fell on his face in the dusty, hard packed ground, dead, his blood mingling with the whiskey in the dim lit alley.

Sheriff Tom Blaine was walking up the sidewalk from the hardware store when he just happened to get a glimpse of a horse at the back door of the Red Horse Saloon.

As he watched, a man came out the door hobbling on a crutch and carrying two bottles of whiskey, putting them into his saddle bag. When he turned to go back inside Tom got a good look at him. Cork Blair! Tom had drawn his Colt and stepped into the alley, waiting, standing in the shadows of the buildings. Well, Cork had his chance, but why would a man risk his life for a bottle of whiskey?

The bartender came out to see what the shots were about. He looked at Cork lying there dead, then at the Sheriff.

"What happened Tom?"

"He wuz too dry an' too slow," the Sheriff told him.

When Bart came in early that evening with a nice fat Spike Buck, he called for Cork to come out and help him skin it. No answer. He went into the cabin. Cork's bunk was empty. Thinking about Cork's need for whiskey as he rolled a smoke, he walked down to the corral in the edge of the Cedars. Cork's horse was gone. Could he have.......,naw! He would not have ridden into town with his bad leg after whiskey. But, he knew his friends weakness for the red liquor, like some men for women or gambling. He could not go very long without it and he knew how Cork had suffered for it the last few days. The damm fool! If he had gone into Rimrock for whiskey let it be on his head. Bart sharpened his knife and began to butcher out the deer.

Late that night a light rain was falling as Jack Sloan led his weary men back to the Box S ranch. The raid had been foiled by extra guards riding on the Wells-Fargo stage that was carrying the twenty thousand dollar strong box. They had helt the stage up, when suddenly the doors of the stage coach sprang open as men leaped out with blazing guns. Buck Sharp, the man who rode in Bart's place was killed and Shad shot up, but still able to ride. They left Buck where he fel,l galloping off Hell bent for leather, barely escaping the withering gunfire.

Jack was sullen and unapproachable while the rest of the men rode in silence. A long wet ride. They stopped at the hideout provided by Jack's friend, dressed Shad's wounds, made coffee, switched horses heading back toward the safety of the ranch. They were a wet, bedraggled, low spirited bunch when they finally got there. Some of the men got Shad to the bunk house and redressed his wounds while the others saw to the horses. Shad's wounds were not too serious, but he had lost a lot of blood.

At ten o'clock next morning sheriff Tom Blaine rode into the ranch yard. Mark Sloan sat on the porch in his wheel chair watching him as he dismounted.

"Whut brings you out this way Sheriff?"

Blaine looked up from tying his horse. "Is Jack hyar Mark?"

"Yeah inside at breakfast. Why?"

Just then Jack Sloan came out the door, staring at the Sheriff with baleful eyes.

"Whut is the trouble Tom?"

Tom got right to it. "Yore man Cork Blair is daid."

Jack's eyed went cold and flat. "Whut happened?"

"I caught him comin' oot of the back door uv the Red Horse Saloon carryin' whiskey. I called fer him tuh turn around an' raise his hands an' when he did his gun wuz in his hand an' swingin' up fer a shot at me. I shot first an' killed him."

Jack's face twisted turning into a mask of hate.

"I do not know anythin' about Cork. The last time I seen him he wuz in yore jail," Jack told him, his voice trembling with rage.

"Yuh knowed him an' Shad wuz broke out."

"I heard about it. Don't matter, cause I wuz gonna fire 'em anyway. I do not want rustlers on my payroll!"

This remark drew a solemn look from the Sheriff. Jack's face looked drawn, hard, a tired look about him, his eyes burned like two coals of fire as he stared at Tom Blaine. And something else on his face, a killing expression, fury, like he was holding himself in check by force of will.

"Wal, yuh hev told me, anythin else Sheriff," he asked in a cold hard voice?

"Not fer the time bein," the Sheriff replied, climbing back aboard his gray horse, and walking him out of the yard.

Jack stared after him and cussed. "Damm it, thet loco Cork died fer a bottle uv whiskey!"

He turned and stomped toward the bunk house. "Bat," he called, "go up tuh the line shack an' tell Bart tuh come on back tuh the ranch. Cork won't need no more lookin' after, cause we gonna bury him tommor!"

At Rocking B, work on the corral and shed was almost finished. Will along with his boys and the new hand, Bud Johns had worked hard as Jim could tell. He had been out on the range with Jesse, Wess and Smoky cutting out the cows and steers they wanted to sell. When they rode in for supper, Jim saw Tom Blaine's horse tied to the hitching rail at the yard gate. Turning his horse over to Smoky, he found Tom sitting on the porch smoking his old black pipe.

"Howdy Jim."

"Evenin' Tom. What brings you out this way, Ann's good cookin'?"

Tom grinned. "Thet would be enuff tuh bring me out, but thar is somethin' else on my mind."

Jim sat down on a bench, and Tom leaned forward.

"I hed tuh shoot Cork Blair yestiddy. He was at the back uv the Red Horse buyin' whiskey. He tryed drawin' on me an' I had tuh kill him, damm the luck, I wanted him alive."

"He came into town for whiskey?"

"Makes no sense atall, does it."

"No, not a bit."

"Wal I rode out tuh tell Jack aboot it an' he said he wuz plannin' on firin' 'em both. He had the look uv a man who had jist seen a big deal go wrong if ever I seen one. Also, I got a telegram frum Captain Jones this mawnin. Thar wuz a holdup in his part uv the country couple weeks ago. The robbers got away with thirty thousand. Three days ago seven men tryed the same thing again. Stage wuz carryin' twenty thousand, but this time they wuz out foxed an' out gunned. The extra guards they carried killed one uv the bandits an' wounded another before they got away."

Here his voice got lower, and he laid a leathery hand on Jim's knee.

"I believe it wuz the Sloans an' some uv thar bunch," he declared.

The old Texan's eyes were gray slits of fire when he uttered the last.

"Do you have anything to go on Tom?"

"Jist a good hunch son. Thet man they killed at the holdup wuz idetified by one uv the guards as Buck Sharpe, who wuz frum thet part uv the country. He worked fer Sloan. Then about two years ago he left hyar after a big argument with Jack at the Red Horse Saloon. My thinkin' is thet he wuz the go between Jack an' whoever is settin' up these holdups. Thet flare up always did hev a shady look tuh me. Now I believe it wuz planned. Jack has always hired rough men, some uv them gunslingers. Thar is four er five workin' thar now thet ain't too fer frum being outlaws."

Jim digested this new information. Tom's hunch might be right.

Just then Ann came out, her face flushed from the heat," supper is ready."

The two men followed her inside the warm kitchen taking seats at the table.

After supper, Tom left for town, leaving Jim something to think about.

Jack was in a foul mood to say the least.

"Yuh think the law might track Buck back hyar," Bill asked?

Jack flung his hand downward splitting the air. "Everybody knows thet I fired Buck off this place two years ago!"

Bill nodded, but still there was doubt. What if somebody had seen him here, although he always rode in and out in the darkness.

Giving his brother a dark glance, Jack stormed off to the bunkhouse. Inside he walked over to where Shad lay in his bunk.

"How yuh feelin' Shad, "Jack inquired?

"Not bad. I will be up an' around soon."

"Sorry I couldn't git yuh to a doctor, but thet would hev brough a lot of questions we don't need."

"Hell Jack, this ain't the first time I been shot. Snap has me patched up pretty good."

Jack shook his head, a gloomy look on his face. After a few minutes he left, the failed job on his mind. The holdup had gone all wrong. Buck killed, Shad shot up. Maybe the holdup business ought to be shelved for a while. They had many thousands of dollars hid away. He began to sort through ideas on how to get his hands on the Rocking B. The first thing was to get rid of Jim Rivers. For now they would stay around the ranch and work cattle here.

For the next couple of weeks, Jim and his crew worked the cattle and he noticed the Box S crew doing the same. He bought twenty head of broke horses from a wild horse hunter he knew and he also got out the old chuck wagon and put on new hoops, canvas, greased the wheels and tightened it up all over. Will Martin's youngest boy Joe, painted it red and yellow. Will and his boys were proving to be a great asset to the ranch. There was no job they wouldn't tackle and do.

Jim rode the boundary lines between the Box S and Rocking B, but nothing out of the way happened. The Box S cattle grazed on their own range and if Jim saw any riders, they were not close. Even though things were smoothing out, he still had that feeling that someone was always watching him. A feeling he had learned not to ignore. He'de had that feeling when he was in Indian country, a shadow on his trail, a feeling of awareness settled over him and he grew more watchful than ever.

At nights he lay in bed with Ann warm and soft beside him, counting his blessings. But in the daylight, the feelings came back to stay with him. Someday the fight between him and the Sloans would come like lighting from the sky. Jim thought of the silver badge he carried in his inside vest pocket. He was to assist Tom in his investigation of the robberys. If something happened down here on the scene, the rangers wanted a man who knew the country and how to handle himself in a fight. He knew Tom was digging into Jack Sloan's business and also checking on some of the men who rode for him. In less than a month they would start the drive taking the cattle to market. He hated to be gone from the ranch for two and a half or three weeks, but he had no choice.

Ann stirred in her sleep and snuggled deeper into the bed next to him, her breathing soft and regular in the darkness. Well, what ever came he would be ready for it. Stealing and hiding the cattle had not brought Sloan the ranch. Maybe if he had not come in answer to Ann's letter, he would have in time. But he knew from his dealing with men over the years that hate never died. So whatever happened he must be ready, always on guard. Finally he closed his eyes and sleep claimed him.

CHAPTER 13

Jack Sloan knew of the cattle drive Jim was planning and instructed his men to stay close to their own range, to let the Rocking B strictly alone.

"I hev a plan fer Rivers an' I don't want anythin' to happen between now an' then tuh put him on guard," he told them.

His henchmen wanted to know what the plan was, but his answer was to wait an' see. There was a hard look in his eyes that boded ill for the Rocking B and Jim Rivers.

One morning while Ann was shopping at Burkes, Jim strolled over to see Tom and check on things.

"JIst the man I want tuh see. Set down Jim," was Tom's greeting.

Jim took a seat lighting a slim cigar; "What's in the wind Tom?"`

"I got a answer tuh some telegrams I sent off. They come in last evening an' might intrest yuh."

"What is in them?"

Bat Smith answers the description uv a bank robber called Bob Short, late uv Utah. Snap Wilson an' Shad Walker wuz paid warriors fer a big cattle outfit up in Montana against the free grazers. Several killin's aire laid at their door. An' guess who Buck Sharpe turned out tuh be."

"One of their old pards."

"Yep. In the same gang uv robbers thet Bat Smith run with."

"I am not surprised Tom."

"The boy who calls hisself the Sundown Kid turns out tuh be a cousin uv Bat Smith. He is a would be gunfighter frum up in Colorado. Killed a couple uv drunks, an' also killed a young boy who bumped into him in the street. Claimed the boy tryed tuh pull a gun on him. The boy wuz never knowed to carry a gun an' they run Sundown out of town. Now thet is part uv the crew Jack Sloan has around him."

"I can remember when I rode for Dave, John had a regular crew of cowboys workin' for him. They was hard and rough, but true cowboys anyway."

"He did Jim, but after he got sick an' took to his bed, Jack started hirin' gun hawks. Most uv the old hands quit, but four er five stuck it out. They do most of the work with the cattle an' mind their own business. The other hands leave 'em alone.

"So, what you are sayin' is that Sloan has two sets of hands."

"Jist what I am drivin' at son. One crew fer the ranch work an' one fer his other business. I remember yuh tellin' me about them seven riders yuh seen up tuh Rock Springs an' it dove tails in with what I have here in these telegrams. They all work together at times, like roundups an' cattle drives, but the everyday work is done by the old hands left thar who wuz with John Sloan."

Jim stared hard at his old friend. "I believe you have hit it square on the head Tom."

"I would bet my gun an' hoss thet I am right Jim. I hev a feelin' in my gut!"

"What do you want me to do?"

"Go ahaid with yore business. Act like nothin' is out uv place. I will keep nosing around an' see whut I kin sniff out. An' by the way, jist between us, I hev talked this over with Judge Barkley an' Kirby White. They aire behind us all the way."

"You told them I am a Ranger?"

"I felt they needed tuh know son."

"Probably for the best Tom."

They stood up then shaking hands warmly.

Jim collected Ann at the store as she said she was done shopping, so he loaded her purchases in the back of the buckboard.

She looked up at him,"could we eat Jim, I am starved."

"Shore, I am hungry myself."

After a big dinner of roast beef, mashed potatoes, beans and apple pie, they were ready to go home. Jim helped Ann into the buckboard, unhitched the team, climbed in and took up the reins. As they passed the Red Horse Saloon, Jack Sloan stood on the wooden sidewalk, his thumbs hooked behind his gunbelt, dark eyes cutting holes through them, a sardonic smile on his red face as he stared at Jim. Ann noticed, but said nothing at the time. As they drove out of town, she looked over at her husband.

"Jim, do you mind if I ask you a question?"

"No, ask me anythin' ."

"I know you led a hard life while you were gone, have you......uh.....have you..."

"Have I killed many men," he asked as he turned and saw her red face?"

She covered her blushing face with her hands.

"The way I have lived over the years Ann, it was kill or be killed, but I am not a killer."

"Oh Jim," she cryed, " I did not mean to imply that you were at all, and I did not mean to pry."

"I will try to explain it to you honey. In the world I lived, it was dog eat dog. I have lived a rough hard life, but I am not callous. There are a lot of bad men in the west an' someone has to stand between them an' the honest hard workin' people, the ones who built this country. Men like your father, uncle an' Tom Blaine. Men who came an' stayed, buildin' somethin', leavin' something behind when they die."

"But the crook, the robber, the thief an' the lustfull tear all that apart. To take what other people have built up. To rob, steal, cheat an' kill without doin' one days hard work. They are the men who men like me have to stand up to an' defeat. Try to make law an' order where there is none. I have always been good with a gun an' so I am not bothered by these low lifes like most other people. They know I can, an' will use a gun, either to protect myself or some other person who is weaker. Yes Ann, I have killed men over the years, but everyone of them deserved it. Is that what you wanted to know," he asked gently?

"Yes," she answered, raising a tear stained face to look at him, her love for him shining in her eyes. "Forgive me Jim, I know your life has been hard and you have had to be hard to survive."

For an answer he put an arm around her and pulled her closer. She laid her face on his strong shoulder drying her tears.

"I love you Jim, very much, and I know it will take a man such as yourself to do the job ahead."

"I love you too Ann," he replied kissing her rosy face.

A light rain set in as they got home, and Jim let Ann out at the yard gate to run to the house while he put the team away. Her purchases could wait until tomorrow to unload. The hands were in the bunk house as he walked by, and there was a card game going on. He hurried into the house to find Ann in her dressing gown, and he knew that was all she had on. He stripped off his wet clothes, rubbed dry with a towel and followed her into the bed room. She turned to him letting her gown slide to the floor, smiling at the expression on his face. They made love that afternoon to the sound of rain on the roof, shutting the world and all it's troubles away. Afterwards they lay together in that soft glow that comes afterward untill slumber claimed them.

The time for leaving on the drive was fast approaching. All the young hands were excited over the prospect, but Jim told them it would be no picnic. But being young they looked forward to anything different than the everyday work around the ranch. Even Smoky was looking forward to it and soon the last week before the drive was here.

One morning just before the drive, while she was cooking breakfast, Ann felt sick. Jim looked over at her from where he sat sipping coffee.

"What is wrong Ann?'

"I don't know, the smell of the bacon frying is making me sick at my stomach."

` Jim got up and helped her to a chair. "Here, sit down," he said gently as he helped her sit.

She did look pale and wan.

"Just sit there an' I will finish breakfast. Do you feel like eatin' anything?"

"No, just some coffee and maybe a biscuit."

He watched as she nibbled at a biscuit, and sipped at her coffee.

"Maybe I should take you in to see Doc Weaver honey."

"No, that's all right. I feel better now."

She seemed to feel better over the next two days, but on the day Jim was set to leave, she told him that she would have to forgo the trip.

"I hate to go off an' leave you here like this Ann."

"Uncle Jesse is here and Wess if I need them, and Barb Martin is just a bit away. I don't think it is anything to worry about. I just don't feel like riding that far and back in that bumpy old wagon."

Jim hugged her to him kissing her soft, warm lips, hating to go, but knowing he must. He strapped on his guns, took up his rifle and opened the door.

"I will go down and see you off," she said.

The cattle were gathered in a field near the house and all the other riders were there, mounted and eager. Smoky sat on the seat of the chuck wagon, now that Ann wasn't going, he was appointed cook and driver. Will Martin and his three boys were there along with Bud Johns. Six riders would be enough to drive the herd of three hundred and forty head. Will had decided to take forty head of his steers along on the drive to sell. They were all waiting for the signal. Jim took his place at the head of the herd and gave that call that had started thousands of cattle over the trail.

"MOVE 'EM OUT."

The herd started moving with the shouts from lusty throats and the drive was on its way. Jim stood up in his stirrups, waved his hat, seeing Ann wave a red scarf. The cattle plodded along raising a cloud of dust. Jesse and Wess stood with Ann watching them leave.

Snap Wilson loped his horse into the Box S ranch yard, where Jack stood on the porch, his hands on his hips waiting. Snap folded a leg around his saddle horn, and reached for the makings.

"They moved the herd out this mornin'."

A wolfish grin turned Jack Sloan's lips up. "Good, good. Now we kin discuss the plan I hev in mind fer Rivers."

Bill Sloan, Bart Short, Bat Smith, the Sundown Kid, and Shad Walker were all at the big kitchen table. Mark Sloan sat nearby in his wheel chair, a bottle of whiskey in his hand. Jack and Snap Wilson came in and took seats as Jack began.

"Rivers an' his crew left out this mornin' drivin' a herd uv cattle tuh Trails End. Snap said there is over three hundred head in thet herd. Figgurin' 'round thirty dollars a head, thet would come tuh seven er eight thousand dollars, er thar abouts. A tidy sum we could use with little work at all."

The men around the table looked at each other.

"Yuh mean fer us tuh rustle them cows an' drive 'em in oure selfs," Bart asked?

Jack laughed, "drivin' cattle ain't my idee at all. Listen. Them buyers at Trails End always pay in cash. They will be packin' thet money with 'em on the way back. We hit 'em as they aire comin' back thinkin' they aire in the clear. The drive will be over an' they will be wantin' tuh git home. We find a good place tuh ambush 'em an' git set thar. Rivers, Smoky an' Martin aire the only men in the crew. Them young fellars will scatter once they hear gunfire. Shad is able tuh ride now an' he has a score tuh settle with Rivers too."

Shad, gunman and back shooter had an evil look on his dark visage as he sat there sipping whiskey.

The drive moved along day by day making twelve to fifteen miles a day. There was good grass and water all along the way. Jim figgured two weeks to get there and five days to get back, pushing hard. He wanted to get back to Ann as soon as possible. He missed her and knew she was feeling the same.

Smoky turned out to be a fair camp cook. The well fed and watered herd was easy to manage. After they were bedded down for the night, two night riders could ride herd on them. Jim and Abe in the first shift, Will and Bud in the last shift before daylight. One night as they sat around the fire after supper, Smoky started talking about his younger days in Texas.

"I knew some uv the gunfighters back then. Bill Hickock, Wesley Hardin, King Fisher, Clay Allison, Bob Lee, an' several more. Seen Wild Bill fight three men one time in Dodge City. Killed all three uv 'em an' never got a scratch. Hardin wuz the wurst. He wuz pizen mean, 'specialy when he wuz drinkin'."

He stared into the flickering fire for a minute, then looked up.

"Nobody 'round hyar knows it, but John Wesley is, er wuz, my cousin."

"He was a mean one all right," Will said, "but I guess we all hev kinfolks like thet some whars."

"Well, time for our watch Abe," JIm spoke up, as he put his coffee cup on a rock by the fire.

The night passed quietly with the bright stars winking down at them, cold and far away while the moon played peek-a-boo through the scattered clouds. In the morning Jim pointed the herd and again, they were under way.

In thirteen days they traveled the one hundred and sixty odd miles to Trails End. They were met at the stock pens by a cattle buyer. After some dickering back and forth, sold out for twenty eight dollars a head. The buyer was a friend of Jim's named Tim Coates.

"You could have got more in Dodge Jim."

"I know Tim, but we needed to make a quick drive an' sale."

"Well boys, we will stay the night here an' see the sights, also I will treat to supper," Jim told his crew.

Will looked at the eleven hundred twenty dollars in his hand, and grinned at Jim.

"Feels good to see some real money in my hand. I am glad for Barb an' the boys Jim, thar aire so many things they need."

"I am glad for you Will, you have a good family. You will all have a months wages due when we get back too."

The young men were standing on first one foot then the other, so Jim gave them some spending money and told everybody to meet back at the hotel at seven for supper. Will took Joe saying there were some things he wanted to buy while they were here. Smoky took off to the saloon for a cold beer, Abe and Bud wandered off in the direction of the huge general store and George went off with Jim to the Blacksmith shop to see about getting a wheel repaired on the chuck wagon.

Before seven they all met at the hotel for supper. They were waited on by a young blonde headed, blue eyed girl who caught Abe and Bud's attention. They were outdone by George, who she seemed to like best. The older men hid their broad smiles behind their hands as they watched the boys. After supper they sat on the hotel porch watching the crowd till bedtime.

The day broke bright and sunny next morning as they headed for the hotel dining room. After an early breakfast, they headed back home. Jim had the money for the cattle, eight thousand and fourty dollars in a money belt around his waist. A fact that weighed on his mind. They made good time on the trail back. Abe, Bud and George drove the remuda along behind the wagon, Smoky driving with Joe on the seat beside him. Jim and Will rode point out in front of the wagon. After a long day they made camp by a shallow willow lined creek, gathering firewood. The boys helped Smoky get supper while Jim and Will took care of the horses. Soon they were seated around the campfire, the smell of frying ham, potatoes and beans filling the air. Biscuits were browning in the dutch oven, coffee was boiling in the pot.

After the meal Jim looked at Smoky and Will.

"It has been a easy drive an' it is not like Sloan to forget about us."

"He ain't fergot Jim," Smoky told him, "I kin feel it in my bones. He will be awaitin' some whars up the trail!"

"I kinda looked fer him tuh stampede the herd," Will said.

"Unless he figgers on doin' it a easier way," Smoky exclaimed.

"I been thinkin' the same thing myself," Jim put in nodding his head. Why stampede or rustle a herd when there is a easier way."

"Like what," Will wanted to know?

"Well, the cattle are sold, an' we are carryin' the money back with us to bank in Rimrock an' holdups are Sloan's trade.

They all stared at him.

"I will be dammed, thet's right," Will exploded.

Smoky cracked a fist in the palm of his other hand. "I will be jiggered! Yuh hit the nail right smack on the head Jim. Tom told me an' Jesse some time back he suspected Sloan uv some robberys up north 'round some uv them minin' camps."

"Smoky," Jim asked,"if you were goin' to hold us up, where would you do it?"

The old cowboy squinted up an eye and smiled, "Rock Crick Pass!"

"Just where I was thinkin', the high rocks there would be a perfect place for a ambush."

"Wal, we caint be shore he will be thar Jim, but we caint take a chance on it."

"How do you want to play it Jim," Will asked leaning forward?

"Here is how we will do it, Listen close."

They all gathered close as Jim explained his plan.

CHAPTER 15

Jack Sloan and his men were in position early on the day he expected Jim Rivers and his crew to return. He had his gunmen scattered among the towering rocks. Each man had a rifle and canteen with him in his hiding place. They were settled in for a long wait if necessary. The horses were hidden back out of sight in a brush choked gully near the creek. Waiting got on the men's nerves and they grew restless, grumbling to themselves. At midmorning, after what seemed like days among the hot rocks, they saw a dust cloud heading their way.

"Thar they come," Jack growled. "Pass the word Snap!"

The little outlaw slipped through the rocks to alert the others.

The wagon and riders came on slowly and Jack Sloan's lips pulled back from his teeth in what might have been a grin, or grimace. Less than a mile out, the wagon and riders stopped as the riders gathered around the chuck wagon. They appeared to be checking the hind wheel on it. Two of them went to a small grove of Willows and began to chop one down. The ring of the axe was clear on the air.

"Whut the Hell," Sloan muttered?

"Looks like they aire liftin' the wagon up fer some reason," replied Snap.

The men below lifted the wagon up with the long pole taking the rear wheel off. As they gathered around the wagon and horses, it was impossible to get a good look at them as no one in the hidden bunch of outlaws had a glass. Two men went back to the grove of trees and the sound of the axe striking wood echoed across the pass.

"Looks tuh me like they broke a axle Jack."

"Damm it Snap, I am tired uv waitin"!

Unknown to Sloan and his band of cut throats, Jim, Smoky and Will were hidden in the rocks below them. They had ridden in there and hid last night. Abe and Bud came with them to take their horses back to camp. Jim and his men were well hidden before Jack Sloan and his henchmen got there in the early dawn. They had watched them hide and marked the places in their minds. Jim had taken a gamble and it had paid off. If they had just rode in unaware, Sloan's ambush would have worked.

Jim reached into his vest pocket, pulled out the Ranger badge and pinned it on. He signaled Smoky and Will as he started to climb out of hidding. They moved forward slowly, silently stalking the bushwackers. The outlaws were positioned so that their backs were toward Jim and his men. They were all watching the group around the chuck wagon as Jim stepped out in plain sight, the sun reflecting off his shiny Arizona Ranger's Badge.

"Hands Up," he shouted as he stood there, a Colt .44 in each hand. The Bushwackers were caught off guard. They turned, getting up slowly to stare at him. Will and Smoky were still hidden out of sight. Jack saw the badge on Jim's chest and laughed like it was a joke.

"Yuh aire a dammed Ranger!"

"Yes, an' all of you are under arrest!"

The surprised men glanced at each other and as one man went for their guns. Jim leaped behind a boulder, both guns blazing. The sound of gunfire increased as Smoky and Will joined in with their rifles. Booms of rifles and sixguns filled the air in the rocks above the creek as gunsmoke hung there like a cloud. Men shot, yelled, cussed and ran, trying to hide from the withering gunfire from the rocks above! For long minutes the sound of battle sounded, fierce, heated, swift, explosive!

Jim punched the empty shells out of his Colts and reloaded as fast as he could. He still had an extra loaded Colt behind his belt at his back, but he was keeping that one for a backup. The sound of drumming hooves caught his ear, turning he saw the dust kicked up by horses stretched out in full gallop. Too far away for a shot! He eased through the scattered boulders his Colts pointing the way. He saw a man stretched out in the dust between two rocks. Creeping up cautiously he moved in, but the man was dead, two blood stained bullet holes in his chest. He heard a sound and wheeled, guns ready, to find Will walking toward him.

"Wal Jim, four of 'em got away, but three wuz too slow," he stated grimly.

"You all right Will?"

"Nary a scratch, but Smoky caught one. Not bad though."

At that point Smoky came up, a bloody bandanna wrapped around his arm.

"As many damm fights as I hev been in, I still cain't seem tuh remember tuh stay down," he complained

"You old rooster," Jim laughed, "let me take a look.

"Jist a scratch Jim, jist a scratch."

Jim had a look anyway. The bullet had passed through the arm just above the elbow missing the bone. Smoky stared at Jim.

"Them four thet got away, one uv 'em wuz ridin' low in his saddle like he wuz hurt."

"Seems tuh me like we come out lucky on this deal Jim," Will remarked.

"Yeah we did at that," Jim agreed. "Signal the wagon an' we will continue on to Rimrock. We ought to get there by early afternoon."

They carried the dead men out to their horses tying them over the saddles. The boys came up with the wagon, staring at the dead men across their horses and the bandage on Smoky's arm.

"You men did good with your part," Jim told them, "an' I am proud of you all."

He sat a fast pace toward town.

Dismounting in front of the Sheriff's office, Jim opened the door and stepped in. Tom looked up, surprised at the badge on Jim's shirt. He stood up quickly knowing something had happened on the drive. Jim explained about the ambush and the three dead men outside. Tom went outside with him to look at the men across the saddles. One by one he raised their heads.

"Bill Sloan, Bart Short, Bat Smith, alias Bob Short. Yuh hev done the county a favor thar Jim," he drawled. "One uv yuh men go fer the undertaker," he told the bystanders.

"I have some business at the bank Tom, an' I will be glad to get shut of this money."

"Come in my office when yuh git back son."

After depositing the money, Jim drew a long breath. They had enough money now to carry them over until the next drive. As he stepped out into the wide street someone called his name.

"Rivers, I been lookin' fer yuh!"

Standing in the street facing him was one of the swaggering gun hawks he had seen hanging around town.

"I am not hard to find."

"Yuh aire worth five hundred dollars tuh me Rivers!"

Jim just stood watching him, a faint smile on his face, relaxed, his hands by his sides. There were two of them around and Jim knew the other one had to be close by. Knowing the game well, he knew the other man would be hidden waiting for his shot. Killers like this always worked in pairs. Nobody paid them any attention because the man had not shouted, but talked in a normal voice. Jim's sharp eyes searched the sidewalks. There, he had the other man spotted. He was in an alley almost across from him. They had him boxed, but this was an old game to Jim Rivers, he had played it many times over the years. As the man in front of him started to draw, the other man would shoot him, then his partner would fire a couple of shots while his friend would withdraw out of sight. A trick that had worked many times.

"The big gun fighter Jim Rivers. I am going tuh kill yuh Rivers an'take yore reputation as the man who killed Jim Rivers."

He wanted to kill Jim, but he wanted to talk first, to tell what a bad man he was, what a fast draw he was. He stood feet apart, his hand quivering over his gun. When he dropped his shoulder to start his draw was when Jim acted. It was something that had saved his life a few times over the years. What happened was so fast it threw every one off guard. Jim dropped to the ground and rolling over, shot the man in the alley, then twisting around shot the man facing him as a bullet kicked up dirt in front of him. The would be gunman struggled to bring his gun up and Jim shot him again. He staggered and fell on his back in the street raising a cloud of dust. People came running then, Tom with them as Jim got to his feet reloading his Colts.

"Whut in the Hell is goin' on," Tom roared, his Colt in his hand?

"They tried to kill me," Jim stated. Had me boxed."

"They," Tom repeated?"

"There is another one over there in that alley. His partner."

Tom went and took a long look and came back putting his gun in it's holster as he shook his grizzled head. "Yuh think Sloan hired 'em Jim?"

"Had to be him Tom, Who else could it be?"

Tom rubbed his chin. "Yeah, who else."

He stood there in thought a minute, then he said. "I am goin' tuh swear in a posse an' head out to Sloan's ranch. I would like fer yuh an' Will tuh ride along."

"Whut aboot me," Smoky piped up?

"Wal if yuh aire able Smoky, I would like tuh hev yuh along."

A dozen strong the posse rode out and when they neared the Sloan ranch spread out in a line. The place seemed to be empty, nobody around as they rode into the ranch yard. They drew rein in front of the porch that ran the length of the house. The screen door pushed open and Mark Sloan rolled out in his wheel chair.

"What is goin' on Tom," he called. When he saw Jim his face darkened.

"Whut in the Hell aire yuh doin' here Rivers," he shouted, half rising out of his chair!

"Hold on thar Mark," Tom cautioned, "Jim is a Arizona Ranger, an' a member uv this posse!"

"Thet killer a Ranger," Mark roared!

"Settle down," Tom told him again. "We aire lookin fer Jack, Snap Wilson an' a few more. Hev yuh seen 'em?"

Some of Mark's anger seemed to drain out of him at the question and he sat back in his wheel chair. "No, not since last night. I went tuh bed an' when I got up they wuz gone."

"Uh huh. Anybody else around hyar beside yuh Mark?"

"Old Lem down at the barn an' the cook an' oure house keeper. Why, what has happened Tom?"

"Jack an' his bunch tryed tuh drygulch Jim an' his crew on thar way back frum the drive."

Mark flashed a hate filled glance at Jim." And?"

"Thar wuz a big fight. Bill, Shad Walker an' Bart Short wuz killed in the shootout. Jack an' three more got away."

"Bill daid." Mark seemed stunned.

Tom dismounted. "We aire gonna search the place Mark."

Help yourself he was told in a sorrowful voice.

A half hour of searching uncovered nothing and the posse mounted up again.

"Wal Jim we aire goin' back tuh town," Tom told him. I need tuh send off some more telegrams."

"An' I need to get home to Ann. The boys should already be there with the wagon an' horses. Ann will be wonderin' about me. If you need me Tom, send word."

"I will son, an' tek caire uv thet pretty little wife of yores," he grinned.

When the posse had been formed, Jim had sent the younger men on home not wanting them to be in danger. As he rode homeward with Smoky and Will, they saw dust coming toward them.

"Whoever thet is on thet hoss shore ain't lettin no grass grow under his feet," Smoky remarked.

As they rode on the rider headed straight for them, only slowing as he got closer.

"Why, thets George," Will exclaimed!

Almost abreast of them the rider brought his hard ridden horse to a sliding, rearing stop. It was George. The sweat rolled down his face leaving streaks through the dust on it.

"Jim,' he panted, "yuh got tuh come quick!"

"What is it George?"

"It's Jack Sloan Jim, he rode intuh the ranch just before we got thar. He shot Wess an' pistol whipped Jesse, an'...an....oh Hell Jim, he kidnapped Miz Ann!"

The words hit Jim like a bullet. His blood froze, then gushed hot through his veins leaving him cold and hard as steel. He put the spurs to Midnight and the big stallion shot forward like an arrow from a bow. His hooves rang on the hard packed road like pistol shots. The wind tore at Jim's face and blurred his sight. Rage flooded his body, fear for Ann tore at him. His face set in a cold hard mask, his eyes slits of gray fire. He thundered into the ranch yard, Midnight's hoofs throwing up dust and gravel as he slid to a stop. Jim leaped out of the saddle before Midnight came to a full stop, a pistol in his hand! Jesse came out of the bunkhouse, a Winchester in his hand, a bloody bandage wrapped around his head.

"Are you all right Jesse," Jim called out?

"Yeah. I will hev a sore head fer a few days though I recon."

"How is Wess?"

"He ain't hit bad. The bullet hit him in the chest, but I think it missed his lung. Went claire through. Looks nasty, an' could be serious. I told George thet after he seen yuh, tuh ride intuh town fer Doc Weaver."

Jim nodded. "What about Ann," he asked in a hoarse voice?

Sloan went up tuh the house an' grabbed her while his men helt guns on me an' Wess an' the boys! They took all the fresh hosses frum the corall an' put Ann up on one. She wuz allright when they left, her sittin' thet saddle like a queen."

"I was goin' to get a fresh horse, but I guess Midnight will have to make it."

"Yuh wont hev tuh worry aboot thet stallion stayin' Jim, he's got fire in him!"

"But listen son, thet ain't all. Sloan said thet if yuh want Ann back unharmed, tuh bring the deed uv the ranch tuh thet old house at Cedar Wells."

"I will be takin' somethin', but it won't be a deed," Jim told him, the words grating like ice rubbing together. He looked as hard and unyielding as Flint Rock, the look of blood lust in his cold gray eyes.

The other young men stood near the bunk house watching.

For the first time Jesse noticed the Rangers Badge on Jim's shirt, and nodded. Jim grabbed the saddle bags off his horse and ran to the house. Quickly he stuffed them full of food and shells. Going into the bedroom he picked up the heavy Sharps from the corner. The fragrance of Ann filled the bedroom and he stood there a long minute, his eyes closed, basking in her scent before he left. Comming back out he laid the saddle bags over the great stallion slidding the big fifty into it's sheath. He turned to Jesse and the others just as Smoky and Will came galloping into the yard.

Will got off his horse and grabbed Jim by the arm. "Wait till I saddle a fresh horse an' I will go with yuh!"

"There ain' no fresh horses Will. Sloan took 'em. Besides, this is my job. It is between Sloan an' me. I don't want to see anybody else get hurt."

Will nodded his head in understanding and squeezed his hand," luck Jim."

Jesse stood by his horse as Jim mounted. "Be kerful son, thet bunch is crazy. When Sloan told me he wuz takin' Ann an' if yuh made it back hyar fer yuh tuh bring the deed, I told him he wuz crazy. Thet's when he hit me with his pistol an' knocked me down. Wess wuz standin' beside me an' grabed fer his gun an' thet damm Shad Walker shot him, then laughed aboot it." The old man looked up at Jim with tears in his faded blue eyes, "bring her back son," he whispered.

Jim gripped his hand in a firm clasp and nodded. Then he was off, Midnight's hoofs clattering on the packed ground. He would bring her back. He knew that Jack Sloan meant to kill him with or without the deed. Jim knew that as surely as he knew anything.

Sloan had finally shown his true colors and he would be like a cornered Lobo now. Jim knew the area around Cedar Wells although he had not been there in years. There was a old log house there that was abandoned when he rode for Rocking B as a youngster. It had been used by different outfits over the years for a line camp. Whoever built it and lived there were long gone and nobody claimed it, though all used it from time to time. There were Cedar trees all around it and a huge one by the well that the place took it's name from. A medium sized spring flowed from under a big moss covered rock back in the Cedars forming a little branch of cold, clear water that flowed down hill and out into the range land. The old house had two large rooms downstairs and one big one overhead. The logs were rotten in places and the old house sagged as if it was tired of standing there over the years. A trail of sorts led up to it.

Dark caught up with Jim before he reached his destination. He made a cold camp by a seep that provided plenty of grass for his horse. After eating a can of beans and a can of tomatoes, he rolled up in his blankets under a dead pine seeking sleep, his thoughts on Ann and the job ahead. Awakening before daylight as was his custom, he brought Midnight in and saddled him. He was moving before the sun came up, chewing on some jerky for his breakfast. When the sun stood overhead he estimated that he was a mile from Cedar Wells and stopped. He unsaddled Midnight staking him out on a long rope so he could graze. He knew Jack Sloan would have a guard on the overgrown trail leading to the old house watching for him, so he would go Indian on them. Digging in his saddle bags he pulled out a pair of soft Moccasins that would make no sound on the ground as he slipped up. He gave Midnight a friendly pat and taking up his Sharps.50 like an old friend, slipped off into the Cedar woods. Sloan had hedged his bet, just in case the two gun hawks in town missed Jim, by kidnapping Ann, the biggest mistake of his life!

The 44-40 Henry was a good dependable gun, but if he got into a tight spot he wanted the extra fire power of the Sharps. His pockets were full of shells for it and his gunbelt was filled also. If they wanted a fight, he would give them one. He slipped through the Cedar woods, their fallen needles lying on the ground like a carpet. There were acres and acres of Cedars in the woods and many of the ranchers cut fence post's here. Every hundred feet or so, Jim stopped to listen peering ahead through the dense cedars. The last time he stopped, there was a smell of cigarette smoke on the air. Someone was close by. He got down on his knees, his eyes searching through the Cedar limbs. There, fifty feet away was the Sundown Kid having a smoke. Jim smiled. It was almost too easy. Slowly he raised the Sharps in line with the Kid's chest. Just then the Kid turned and looked straight at him. He seemed frozen for a moment, then with a strangled cry went for his gun. Jim was in no mood to try talking to him about surrendering. The big bore Sharps was already in line with him as Jim caressed the trigger. The Sundown Kid's feet flew out from under him like he had been hit by a giant hand and he went backwards sliding in the leaves to lay there sprawled out unmoving, a big hole in his chest. No need to check him, Jim had seen dead men before. Sliding a fresh cartridge in the breech of the Sharps, he started for the sway backed house up ahead!

CHAPTER 16

Sloan and his desperate men rode into the ranch yard of the Rocking B before anyone knew they were there with drawn guns. They helt the two old men and the others under them.

"Sundown, Snap, saddle us some fresh hosses. Shad keep a eye on these two," he ordered!

Shad had an evil look on his face as he stood with two black Colts on Jesse and Wess. He looked as if he would like one of them to make a move. Snap hobbled off with Sundown, a bloody bandanna around the upper part of his right leg and one around his head. He was not in a good humor either. Jack ran toward the house, to return shortly leading a white faced Ann. Sundown and Snap were there with the fresh horses now staring at her. He told her to keep quiet. There was a strange expression in his dark fierce eyes and at that moment, Ann knew he was unstable. She decided to humor him.

"Yuh come with us quiet like an' I won't shoot these two," he growled, waving his gun at the men there, standing with their hands in the air. Understand? Do yuh need anythin' frum the house?"

"My riding outfit and my coat."

"Lets go git 'em."

He followed her into the house and on into her bedroom.

"Please, I need some privacy to change."

Jack searched the room for any kind of weapon.

"I will not try to trick you," she told him pleadingly.

He stepped from the room standing just outside the door. Ann made the quickest change of her life with him standing there and grabbing her coat came out. She stood there quietly as Jack looked her over.

"Come on, we gotta ride," He said, grabbing her by the arm.

The other men stood by the horses, waiting. Sloan strode over to Jesse.

"I want yuh tuh give Rivers a message fer me, if he gits hyar. Tell him thet if he ever wants tuh see his pretty little wife again, fer him tuh bring the deed fer this ranch tuh me at Cedar Wells in two days, er else she will dissapear! Understand!"

"Sloan, yuh aire crazy," Jesse spat at him.

Sloan whipped out his pistol and slashed Jesse across the head with it. With a cry Ann started toward her uncle, but Sloan jerked her back. Wess thinking he saw his chance then, went for his gun, and Shad shot him. The old man fell to the ground with a grunt. Ann cryed out almost fainting at the sight of her old friends and companions lying there on the ground, bloody and beaten. Rough hands grabbed her and sat her in the saddle. Hands tied in front of her, Sundown led her horse out of the yard. She looked back with tear dimmed eyes until they were out of sight.

They rode for what seemed like hundreds of miles until she thought she would surely fall out of the saddle. The sharp smell of Cedar reached her nostrils and the horse's hoofs made no sound now as they rode through the trees. It was long after dark when they reached the old log house. She was lifted out of the saddle and led inside, where one of the men lit a candle. The tiny flickering light it threw out making shadows on the walls. Soon Shad had a roaring fire of Cedar knots blazing in the crumbling rock fireplace. The Cedar faggots threw a cheerful light over the gloomy room. Ann's hands were untied and she lay down on one of the musky bunks there along the far wall, not caring how bad it smelled. She was bone tired in both body and spirit. Shad seemed to be the cook of the outfit as he sliced bacon into a large iron skillet dumping several cans of beans into another. From a large pack in the corner, he took out a loaf of stale bread and going to the well, drew a bucket of the cold water. Then he filled the coffee pot setting it near the fire to boil.

The pack had been sat there a few days after Jack planned the ambush of Jim Rivers. He knew they would have to disappear for a while after that. But now, the plan had changed. The money from the robberys was packed in saddle bags that now lay under the rickety table where he sat. When he had the deed to the Rocking B signed over to him, he would go to Mexico, sell the ranch through a laywer, then he would have Mark sell the Box S and come down to join him and the others. With all that money they could live like kings for the rest of their lives. Jack had big schemes and dreams. He thought it would be easy to do all that, but his warped mind did not comprehend things clearly. The thought of killing Jim and Ann did not bother him at all. In his world he was right, his plans worked, he could escape the law. Things were not right or wrong to him, they were as he wanted them to be. If the two so called gunslingers didn't get Rivers, he would follow them here. If the gunmen did get Rivers, he would make Ann sign over the ranch to him and she would just disappear.

Ann lay on the dirty bunk, too tired and overwrought to sleep. In her mind's eye she could still see Uncle Jesse and Wess laying on the ground bloody, limp, unmoving. Jim would come for her. She knew he was on her trail, that he would never stop until he found her and made her safe. She thought of his strong, rugged features, his gentle ways toward her, his love for her. Those thoughts were interrupted by Jack Sloan's rough voice.

"Hyar, eat this."

She sat up and he handed her a plate of the beans and bacon, a piece of the stale bread and a cup of strong coffee. Ann was not hungry, but she knew she had to keep her strength up. Choking down the food, she sipped on the hot black coffee. It seemed to revive her somewhat. She had already decided not to make any trouble, or say too much. Finishing her megar meal, she lay back on the lumpy bunk and drifted off to sleep dreaming of Jim. Across from her in another bunk Snap Wilson lay in an uneasy sleep. He had been lying there ever since they arrived at the house.

Sun shining through a hole in the chinking between the weathered logs woke Ann. For a minute, she didn't remember where she was, then she heard Jack's voice and remembered. The smell of coffee and frying ham floated on the air, and she found that she was hungry this morning, starved in fact. When it was ready she was called to the table to sit down on a box at one end of the rickety table. In spite of the situation she ate heartily of the ham and bread, drinking two cups of the strong black coffee. After eating, Jack called Sundown outside where there was a heated argument for a few minutes, then Jack came back inside, a wild look in his eyes. All the morning he seemed jumpy to Ann, going to the door often to look down the overgrown road. Shad sat at the table and smoked, his eyes darting back and forth from Jack to her, a deck of greasy cards in his hands. Shad had put a kettle of beans and bacon on the fire after breakfast and now he brought the small kettle over and sat it on the table. Just as he sat them down there was a faint boom. Jack ran to the door and Shad jumped up, jerking out his .45 Colt to stood beside Jack who also had a gun in his hand.

Snap sat up in his bunk staring around and his fever seemed to have broke during the night. "Hey, how about a cup uv thet coffee."

Jack and Shad turned to look at him.

"Good tuh see yuh up Snap," Jack said. "How yuh feelin'?

"Better this mawning. I am hungry". He got up out of the bunk and made his way to the table.

Jack pointed at Ann. "Fix him some grub, then check them wounds."

She did as she was told. Snap ate two slices of the leftover ham, some of the fried bread, a bowl of the beans and drank three cups of coffee laced with whiskey. After he was through, Ann checked his wounds. They were a little inflamed, but not swollen. She redressed them and the little outlaw stood up and buckled on his guns.

"Yuh think thet wuz a shot we heerd a while ago Shad?"

"Sounded like a shot tuh me Jack.

"Thet must uv been what woke me up," Snap told them.

"Rivers," Jack hissed. "He is here!"

Dinner was forgotten by Jack and Shad, and it sat on the table getting cold. The two men stood poised like deer, listening and watching. Snap sat smoking, cleaning his guns. Ann felt her heart beat faster, Jim was here! She lay on the bunk hardly breathing hoping the men would forget about her.

Jack looked at Shad. "Go see about the Kid!"

"If Rivers is hyar an' thet wuz his shot, thar ain't no use goin' tuh see about the Kid. He has done been seen about."

"Proably right," Jack agreed. He had an unstable look about him. His eyes holding a crazed expression, the stare of a fanatic. The hate boiled out of him. Somewhere along the line, Jack's mind had slipped.

"We will fix Rivers," he told Shad.

He stepped outside. "Rivers," he bellowed, "if yuh aire here answer me!"

"I hear you Sloan!"

"We got yore woman hyar!"

"That is why I am here Sloan, to get her and kill you!"

"Wal if yuh want her, bring thet deed up hyar an' git her!"

"Here I come Sloan!"

Slowly Jim walked out of the Cedars toward the sagging old house. It was more run down that he remembered. Most of the chinking had fallen out from between the logs. The big chimney leaned away from the house and some of the top rocks had fallen off, but judging by the smoke coming out of the top of it must still be working. He walked carefully toward the three men watching him. His hands hung loosely by his sides near the Walnut handled Colt .44's. When he was thirty feet away, he stopped.

"Did yuh bring the deed Rivers," Sloan asked?

"Let me see Ann first."

Sloan made a movement with his hand. Shad went in and brought her out.

She smiled at Jim, "I knew you would come."

"Are you all right Ann?"

"Yes Jim, I am all right."

Shad took her arm and walked her back inside.

"Now thet yuh hev seen her, let me see the deed," Sloan demanded.

"It is in my pocket," Jim said.

"Wal, dig it out then," Sloan ordered, moving his hand closer to the bone handled .45 on his left side that was set for a cross draw.

Very carefully Jim reached into his shirt pocket and brought out a large folded piece of paper slowly unfolding it.

"Git it Shad," Sloan told him, his eyes on Jim.

When they came out Jim saw the bandage on Snap Wilson's arm and noticed that he was limping. He was the one of the four that got shot, but his eyes were watchful, like a rattle snake. Jim knew he was in one tight place. He faced three guns and his and Ann's life hung in the balance. He must work this just right.

As Shad started forward, the paper slipped from Jim's hand and fluttered to the ground. When he bent over to pick it up, he suddenly dropped to one knee and made that fast draw he had practiced for years. Jim knew he had to get Snap first for he was the original dyed in the wool gunman! Snap was caught off guard as was Jack and Shad. They had expected him to talk, maybe even plead a little, but they knew very little about the character of Jim Rivers. He was outnumbered and drawing on them was the last thing they expected him to do.

Jim's guns were firing as Snap's were coming up. One of Jim's bullets hit him in the chest, another in the shoulder. The little gunman was fast and hard to kill. He got off two shots before a bullet from Jim's gun pierced his heart. He half turned, crumpled and fell to the ground. Sloan and Shad were shooting now, one of their bullets clipped Jim's side. He rolled over scrambling to his feet as another bullet hit his leg causing him to stagger and fall. Sloan had another gun out now and both he and Shad were blasting away at Jim. The loud boom of a rifle was heard just as Jim got his feet under him, his Colts hammering into Sloan. The rifle bullet hit Shad just as he trained his guns on Jim. Shad staggered and the rifle roared again, driving him backwards and down on his back to lay there unmoving. The hard hitting slugs from Jim's Colts had Sloan reeling but still he shot at Jim, his shots going wild. A terrible roar came from deep in his chest, wild with pain and hate. Jim emptied his Colts into him, walking in, shooting with both hands. Jack Sloan was shot to doll rags but still he stayed on his feet, swaying drunkenly in a half circle, then tottering, he fell face down in the grass still holding his guns. Jim reached behind him for the spare Colt, but saw he would not need it. As Jim began to reload, he heard a call and turned to see Will Martin striding forward, a Spencer .56 in his hands.

"Thanks Will. Good to see you!"

Will stared down at what was left of Shad Walker. "Owed it tuh him. He shot a good milk cow fer me one time. No reason fer it atall."

Ann came running out then, her hair flying, her eyes wide.

"Jim, oh Jim, I knew you would come."

She flew into his open arms, hugging, kissing, laughing, and crying at the same time.

"Hope you wasn't scared Ann."

"I watched the whole thing through a hole between the logs." Then she stopped and drew back. "Jim, you're hurt."

He looked down at the blood on the leg of his jeans and felt a pain in his side where a bullet had creased him.

"Come inside and I will bandage it for you darling."

"While you are fixin' Jim up, I will search these hombres an' see what they got on 'em," Will said.

Inside Jim sat in a chair drinking coffee while Ann cleaned and bandaged his wounds. The bullet had gone through the fleshy part of his leg, a clean wound. The one on his side was sore as Hell. The bullet had hit a rib, followed it around and come out tearing a jagged hole. Although they were not that serious, they needed tending and would require a Doctor when they got home. Ann washed them out with hot water, and wetting a strip of cloth with whiskey sterilized them, making Jim wince. She tore off a strip of her petticoat to bind them up with. Jim took a serious drink of whiskey for the pain. He looked up at Ann's white face as she tied the bandages.

"Did they hurt you Ann," he asked softly?

She looked into his eyes. "No, they hardly noticed I was here, although it was a long hard ride for someone in my condition."

"Condition, are you sick?"

"Well no, not really. I went into town after you left to see Doc Weaver, and.....

"An' what, tell me Ann!"

"When I said condition, what I meant was, I am going to have a baby Jim."

He took her by the hands, "you gonna have a baby?"

Jim sat there with his mouth open.

"Say something Dear."

"I am just so happy, I am speechless honey."

He pulled her onto his lap. "My life is complete."

She put her arms around his neck. "Jim, did you really bring the deed to the ranch?"

He showed her the paper and she laughed. "Why, this a bill of sale for the cattle."

She gave him a kiss then that he felt clear down to his toes. The sound of horses pulled them apart and Jim went to the door, hands on his Colts. He turned to Ann.

"It is Tom and some of the hands."

He hobbled outside to greet them.

"Wal", Tom said looking at the three men on the ground, "looks like the fun is over."

"Had it not been for Will, the outcome might have been different," Jim told him.

"I wuz worried about yuh, so I hit yore trail. Almost got hyar too late" Will said.

"Right on time Will, right on time."

"Say Tom, take a look at whut I found on Sloan," Will said, handing him a heavy leather wallet.

Inside was thousands of dollars plus a letter from a man in Colorado, a lawyer called Clem Dall, telling of a shipment that would be of interest to them both.

"I will send this tuh Cap Jones at Ranger headquarters. Thet will clear up a lot of questions fer him."

"Recon we ought tuh bury these fellars'," Will told them.

"Yeah, worms got tuh eat too," Jim said.

Theyburied the outlaws there beside the old rotting house, laying their guns and other belongings in a pile by the kitchen table.

Tom got the money from the saddle bags laid them on the table and they gave it a rough count. He looked up at them.

"A fortune in stolen money," Tom exclaimed. Wells-Fargo will be glad tuh git this back, 'cause all uv it come frum robbin' thar stages. Also thar is a reward fer the robbers, an' the return uv the money." He glanced at Jim who shook his head.

"Give half of it to Will, an' the rest to the Rockin' B crew Tom. They deserve it after all they been through."

There were big smiles as the boys looked at each other. Loading up everything on the spare horses, they started back to Rocking B without a backward glance.

People avoided the old sagging house at Cedar Wells after that, saying it was haunted by the ghosts of the outlaws killed there. The old house weathered more over the years, finally falling down into a pile of rotten logs and fire blackened stones. The things that had happened here over time, good deeds and bad, were forgotten, as weeds and small trees claimed the place where the old house had once stood.

A year had passed since the fight at Cedar Wells and a baby Jim Rivers had arrived at Rocking B much to the joy of all. The ranch was now running nearly four thousand head of cattle and Jim had Will's boys riding for him along with Bud and two other young men. The three old hands still spent some time in the saddle, passing their knowledge on to the younger hands. Jim was no longer a Ranger, devoting his time to his family and the ranch. Mark Sloan had sold his ranch and moved away, nobody seemed to know where.

Jim didn't carry two guns anymore, but he always kept one handy. Some days Ann rode the range with him for Jim had hired a woman to help her with the house work so they could have more time together. They laughed remembering the day he had come home to her and she had asked him to marry her to save the ranch. Their lives were full and rich. Jim Rivers had come home to stay...

THE END.

BROTHER'S OF THE GUN.

The soft night wind off the high hills above him waved the dark black hair on the back of his neck as he sat there looking off into the distance. The rider patted his horse's shoulder, then withdrew a long slim cigar from his vest pocket. Striking a match with his thumb nail, he lit up, inhaling the strong smoke, slowly letting it out in a small cloud. Lights from a not too distant town showed in the prairie lands ahead. The winking lights looked soft and inviting to him after his long ride. Touching his mount again, he spoke softly into the dark night.

"He is down there Sun. There is a range war gettin' ready to start and he will be caught right in the middle of it. He wouldn't want my help, or ask for it, but he will get it anyway. It will be for his wife an' son also. Too proud an' stiff necked for his own good." The man on the big Red Stud chuckled," but I am goin' to help him an' back him all the way, whether he wants me an' my guns or not. She is down there too Sun, I know she is. It has been a few years since we have seen each other an' I will shore be glad to see her again. Never should have left her like I did, but she understood the reason for it. Course she might be married by now. A beautiful woman like her has a lot of men wantin' to look after her. Just have to keep my guns loose an' see what happens down there. See how the hand plays out," he told his horse, a bright red Sorrel sixteen hands high and the color of the setting sun. Sun twitched his ears and stamped his right front hoof, shaking his head causing his bridle to rattle. The rider chuckled and patted his sleek neck fondly, then lifting the reins, rode out of the foot hills and on toward the town of Twin Rivers.

Riding down the wide main street he walked Sun over to the livery stable dismounted tiredly. A young, skinny man in bib overalls came out staring at the tall rider in black, "yes sir?"

"Rub him down good, give him a bucket of oats an' plenty of hay," the tall man instructed, flipping him a five dollar gold piece. The stable man caught it in the palm of his hand and grinned. "Yes sir, bucket of oats an' plenty hay."

It was nearly ten o'clock when the tall rider entered the Cattleman's Hotel, his saddle bags over his left shoulder and a Winchester 44-40 in his right hand. He rang the bell on the desk, waking the night clerk who was napping in an overstuffed chair behind it. The old man opened his eyes, blinking at the sudden light, getting up slowly to lean on the edge of the desk.

"Help you sir?"

"Need a room for a while", he was told.

"Yes sir. Sign here."

The old man turned the register book around so the tall man with the two dark tied down Colts could sign it. The clerk took in the guns, the black flat brimmed hat, dark jeans and the blue shield fronted shirt. The clothes were dust covered and showed long travel stains. The man himself seemed tired, almost weary as he signed his name. Only the guns looked clean and well cared for. Another gunhand come to town the old man thought. Handing the stranger a key, the clerk pointed to the stairs.

"Room twelve sir, top of the stairs on the right Mr.....,"he craned his neck to read the signature in the book.., Cooper."

Mr Cooper nodded laying some money on the counter as he picked up the key to his room. "Thanks, let me know when that runs out friend."

The clerk picked up the coin and looked at it, turning it over in his hand. "Good fer three nights Mr Cooper. Will you be stayin' with us long sir?"

"Depends on the weather around here," the answer floated back over a shoulder.

He made his way up the stairs, found his room and unlocked the door. Inside he lit a lamp sitting on the scratched and faded dresser, then relocked the door, putting a chair under the knob. He removed his vest and hat, took off the twin Colts and laying them on the bed, took off his dirty shirt. Pouring tepid water from the pitcher into a bowl sitting there, he washed most of the trail dust off his face and upper body. The cake of soap was small, but he made do. Tomorrow he would find a barbershop and laundry, if there was one, have his clothes washed along with a hot bath, shave and haircut. Completing his meager bath, he sat on the side of the bed and removed his boots, frowning at a hole in one of his socks. No doubt about it, he needed to buy some new clothes. Taking off his pants, he sat back down washing his feet as best he could. The blinds were drawn in the small hot room. He pulled one back, peering down at the street below. It was quiet, but then this was the middle of the week. He put the blind back in place, blew out the coal oil lamp and lay down in the lumpy bed stretching out his tired body. He slipped one of his Colts under the flat pillow, yawned and went to sleep.

Mr Cooper awoke at the first sign of daylight as he had every morning since he was a boy. As he dressed, the sounds of a waking town sifted up to him. The screaking of a well pump. A proud hen announcing to the world that she had lain another egg. A late sleeping rooster crowing at the rising sun. Somewhere a dog barked, a door slammed and a team of horses pulled a wagon down the street, it's wheels complaining about the lack of grease. Strapping on his guns he settled his hat on his head to suit him, leaving the stale room, making his way downstairs for breakfast.   His eyes took in everyone in the lobby before he stepped off the stairs. Several people were in there waiting for the hotel dining room to open. They glanced at him nodding as he crossed the lobby to take a seat. A drummer sat in a chair reading a five day old newspaper. He glanced up, took a look at the twin tied down Colts, going back to his paper. Mr Cooper was a stranger here, but no one seemed to pay him any undue attention.

In just a few minutes the dining room doors opened and the people started filing inside finding seats. Mr Cooper nodded to the men, tipping his hat to the women as they passed him. They all nodded back. He took a seat at a corner table, his back to the wall from long habit formed over the years. A pretty young girl with pale blond hair, blue eyes and freckles across her pert nose came over to take his order.

"Ready for breakfast sir," she asked in a cherry voice?"

"What do you have this mornin' miss," he asked, smiling up at her.

"Ham or steak, fried potatoes, biscuits, eggs, and gravy."

"Bring me the ham an' everything else, an' keepin' my coffee cup filled will earn you a nice tip," he grinned.

"Yes sir," she laughed and whirling, headed for the kitchen where all kinds of good smells wafted through the open door. She was right back with his coffee.

He sat back in his chair enjoying the hot, strong coffee and studying the crowd there. By the time he had emptied his coffee cup, the waitress was back with a refill plus a heaping plate of food, the smell making his mouth water. She left to return with a small plate of biscuits and Mr Cooper dug in. It smelled good and tasted even better. The young, smiling waitress saw to it that his cup stayed full. He finally pushed his plate back with a satisfied sigh, full to his eyeballs. He was so full that he hardly had room for a toothpick. There was another girl serving on the other side of the room that favored the one that had served him and he knew they had to be sisters. He settled back with a slim cigar feeling at peace with the world. The smiling waitress came by to collect his dirty dishes and he paid his bill, giving her a fifty cents tip. She dropped the money into her apron pocket.

"Thank you sir. Come back and eat with us again," she smiled.

"I will do that young lady," he told her.

He rose from his chair, strolling out on the hotel porch. Finding a comfortable rocking chair, sat down in it to enjoy his cigar and get the feel of the town. The streets were busy with wagons, buckboards, saddle horses and folks going about their daily business. Three cowboys rode by at a slow walk as if they had all day to get somewhere, the brands on their horses was the Bar O. Must be Owen Straight's outfit. Straight owned or claimed all the land east of town just as Sam Barton claimed all the land west of town. Barton's Box B was running short of water so he was eyeing Straight's side of the fork. The town of Twin Rivers sat right between the Forks and right smack dab in the middle of the trouble that was coming. And it was coming. Mr Cooper could feel it. He had been in many such wars over the years with his guns hired out, but he had always fought on the side of right. When it did come, the Sheriff would be caught in the middle, between the pinchers of the two big ranches. For some reason, Red Rock River split into two forks after leaving the mountains where it was born and the town lay in the forks. Barton's West Fork was slowly drying up as the weather grew hotter, but Straight's East Fork was still running full blast. The town was full of deep wells that never went dry, so had no worries about water, but Barton was casting a lustful eye towards the East Fork. When a man's cattle get thirsty, he gets mighty edgey and many a range war had started over water.

Barton had gotten it in his head that Straight had somehow diverted the water over to his side. Straight told him point blank that he was crazy and warned him away from the East Fork or suffer the consequences. They had been feuding over it for the last three months and every time the two outfits met in town, there was a fight. Last time one of the Bar O cowboys had been shot in the shoulder by one of the Box B crew. The man called Cooper could almost smell the gunsmoke, knowing in his mind from long experiance that soon there would be plenty of it. The small fights would erupt into a full scale range war, dragging everyone in town into it. He would sit and watch, bidding his time until he was needed. That he would be needed was clear to him, if not to others.

Looking down the street he saw a woman crossing and even at that distance he knew who it was. It was her. Shannon O'donnel. No other woman had that regal walk. She carried herself like a Queen. He knew her every mood and feature. The way she had of holding her head when she talked. Her musicial laugh. The flashing green eyes. The thick red hair. The firm body beneath her clothes that was all woman. Shannon! He finished his cigar and rising from his chair, started a slow walk around town nodding or speaking to everyone he met. He walked slowly by the jail. Peeking through the window on his slow walk, he saw the Sheriff sitting at his desk, a pile of papers in front of him. It had been a few years, but he looked the same. Sheriff Lee Coulter. He smiled to himself and thought of going in, but that could wait, no rush to reveal himself just yet. Coming to a large saloon he pushed the bat wing doors open and walked inside, slipping to one side so his eyes could adjust to the dim light. The room was cool inside, smelling of stale beer and smoke. He leaned on the bar and ordered a beer. The bartender served him, scooped up the coin, and continued wiping the bar. With his elbow on the bar, Mr Cooper sipped at his beer and looked around the large room of the Crystal Palace.

The saloon had a long polished bar with a footrails and spitoons. Behind it was a giant mirror with paintings hanging around it. It was clean and orderly in there and it appeared to be a classy place. There were card tables and over by the window was a wheel of chance. Even at this time of day there were several men playing poker at a couple of the tables. Everything in there had that well cared for look, clean and orderly. A winding staircase led to the upstairs and rooms there. He would come back later tonight when a crowd would be there. A saloon was always a clearing house for news and information. Where men gathered to drink and gamble, they talked and he aimed to listen. He strolled out the swinging doors starting back towards the hotel and his comfortable chair there. Walking past the rambling general store, he glanced inside. There she was by the counter paying for her purchases. The same flaming red hair and flashing green eyes he remembered so well. For the second time that day, he felt the urge to go to her and take her in his arms. But somehow he decided not to, and walked on by. Soon everybody would know who he was, that he was staying in town, but they would not know the reason why he was here. That was his secret. Something he would keep to himself for the time being. One other man might guess, or know why he was here, but by then it would not matter. He would complete his mission and fulfill a promise made years ago. How long it took him to keep that promise did not matter. He had nowhere to be and none to grieve for him if he was killed fullfilling that promise. Mr Cooper felt alone and a strange feeling came over him, a melancholy feeling that washed over him like a cold chill.

He was a lonely man, a drifter, a fast gun for hire. He would die alone some day in a strange dusty street of some unknown town such this. His gun would hang in it's holster, or he would meet a faster gun, someone wanting to build a reputation. There would be no one to cry over him, to miss and remember him. No wife or son to carry on his name when he was gone. Other men would breathe a sigh of relief after he was dead. He sat down in a chair on the hotel porch, wiping the sweat from his face. A shutter ran through his body like someone had stepped on his grave. He needed to leave some mark of his passing, something to be remembered for and that was why he was here in Twin Rivers. What he had in mind doing might cost him his life, but at least it would be for a good cause, a promise kept! Mr Cooper sat there thinking back over his life. When had he ever really had a chance to be anything other than what he was?

Once he had been a young cowboy of eighteen living in West Texas and the world lay at his feet. Then, his world as he knew it came crashing down around him. That was the day the outlaws came to the ranch. They raided the ranch, stealing a herd of cattle and some horses, but worst of all, killing his Aunt and Uncle. He was on the far side of the ranch rounding up some strays when it happened, too far away to hear the gunshots. When he rode in later that day, he found his Aunt and Uncle lying in the yard dead. It was twenty miles to town, so he buried them with tears in his eyes, a hot knot in his chest. Standing by the graves he read over them from Aunt Matty's faded Bible, and hung his Uncle Frank's hat on the rough cross at the head of his grave. He stood there, the rage in him burning out the tears from his gray eyes. Closing the Bible, he went into the house, up to his room. Kneeling by an old Oak chest, he dug down in the bottom of it and came out with another Colt .44, and two boxes of shells. He got two shirts and a pair of jeans from the dresser and came down to the kitchen. Rummaging through the cabinet, he laid some jerky, coffee and sugar on the table beside the boxes of shells. He also got a frying pan, salt and a coffee pot. Carrying all this outside he filled his saddle bags climbing aboard the bay horse standing there waiting for him. With one last look at the fresh graves, he rode out of the yard without a backward glance.

His uncle Frank had been a scout for the army in his younger days and showed Harlan how to track on the ground and also in his mind. A man tracking someone learns a lot about the man he is tracking by the way he rides and sets up his camp. He was good with his hands and drawing a gun just came naturally. He was fast with a gun and had never known fear of anything. Now these things would come in handy. Finding their trail he soon separated the tracks of each rider so he would know them from any others. Harlan tracked them for two days and they seemed to be slowing down. Fear of pursuit did not seem to bother them.There was five different sets of tracks and each one of them was imprinted in his mind. The third day he knew he was catching up to them. Later that day, he heard cattle bawling ahead. Tying his horse, he slipped through the trees and scrub brush locating their camp. He watched for a while as they got comfortable, letting the tired cattle graze. Going back to his horse, he waited until dark, then he mounted and rode toward the outlaw's camp. He walked the Bay, it's movement making only a slight swishing sound in the grass. When he was close, he put the reins in his mouth, drew both Colts and charged.

He caught them off guard as he thundered in with both Colts blazing away. One of the men was standing near the fire, a cup in his hand, when Harlan rode into the camp scattering them and putting two bullets into the standing man. Quickly he swung his horse charging back through the camp again, shooting a man by the fire raising a rifle at him three times, then rode out like a flash, a wild yell floating behind him. The other two men by the fire emptied their guns at him, never even getting close. The last man out riding herd on the cattle heard the gunshots. When he came galloping in the other two almost shot him. "Whut in the Hell is goin'on", he yelled. He soon found out. Early next morning the rustlers moved the herd out at a fast pace leaving two freshly dug graves behind

Harlan had them spooked now and hounded their trail for two days like an Indian until he got a chance to shoot again. They were driving the horses ahead of the cattle with only one man riding drag. Harlan crept up on him untill he was close enough, then threw his old Henry rifle up and shouted at the man, who turned and jerked at his gun. The big Henry knocked him out of his saddle and Harlan threw a few shots at the other two, wounding one of them. They tore out shooting back over their shoulders, but now he had their tracks and faces in his mind and he would catch up with them sooner or later. He gathered up the cattle and horses starting them for a town up ahead called Texas Junction, a cattle town on the railroad. There was always a cattle buyer around there, and that was where he headed.

Driving a herd of two hundred cattle and fourteen horses was a Hell of a job for just one man but he did it. Six long, hot, dusty days later he drove them down the main street of Texas Junction and up to the cattle pens there by the railroad tracks. A young long legged man ran to open the gates for him. Three of the horses wore saddles. Tied to the saddles and in boots were the rustler's guns. The Sheriff came down to the cattle pens and Harlan told him his story as several other folks gathered to listen. The Sheriff said he could do as he wanted with the rustler's horses and guns. One of them was a brand new Winchester.44-40 and one of the Colts was also new. Harlan decided to keep them for himself as well as one of the horses, a long legged Buckskin. Soon the story would be all over town, but all Harlan wanted was a hot bath, a shave and some sleep.

He sold the cattle and horses to Ben Dobbs, a cattle buyer from Kansas City, putting the check for them into the town's bank for safe keeping. The money could be transferred from there to the bank in Black Buttes where his other Aunt lived. He was glad his younger brother had been staying with her going to school when the outlaws hit the ranch. People of the town stared at the tall young man in the dusty clothes and batwing chaps, loaded down with guns as he made his way tiredly into the hotel lobby. He got a room there, asking for a tub of hot water. The hotel had a wash room at the back so he went there, stripped down, and soaked for half an hour, then shaved, put on cleaner clothing, making his way up the stairs almost stumbling into his room. He locked the door behind him and crawled into bed, asleep before his head settled on the pillow.

He slept for twenty hours before rising and felt groggy then. Getting up, he went to the dresser pouring warm water from the pitcher with the pictures of roses on it into a matching bowl. After washing his hands and face he felt better. He combed his dark hair and dressed in fresh clothes, finding that he was starving. Most of his meals the past two weeks were coffee and jerky, or a can of beans. Buckling his guns on, he sat his old brown Stetson on his head, left his room and went out and down the stairs. He found that he had gained a reputation of sorts. Folks on the street talked to him like he was Bill Hickok. At the restaurant where he ordered four eggs, fried potatoes and a big steak, the men sitting around in there asked him all about the drive and he told them he was just doing his duty to his Aunt and Uncle who raised him and his little brother. Several of them clapped him on the back and told him it was one of the dammtest deals they ever heard of. A few young ladies caught his eye with shy glances and one of the older ladies batted her eyes at him and smiled. After finishing his meal, he walked down to the Sheriff's office to talk to him. The Sheriff, Bob Miller, had sent off some telegrams after Harlan brought in the stolen cattle and horses. Now he showed the answers to Harlan.

"Men answerin' the description uv the ones yuh shot may be part uv the Clements gang, fer thet is the way they operate. Ride in, shoot everybody an' steal cattle an' hosses tuh drive off an' sell. The two thet got away sound like Sam Clements an' his brother Jed. They been raidin' 'round this part uv the country fer some time. Never been caught 'cause they leave no witness's."

Harland thought that over shaking his head. He stood and shook hands with the Sheriff. "Thanks for everythin' Sheriff. I will be keepin' a eye peeled for them an' if I see 'em, I will put my brand on 'em."

"Luck son," Miller told him. "Watch yore back trail."

After a couple more days of rest and eating, he headed back to Black Buttes, and what was left of his home. Frank and Matty Cooper had taken him and his little brother in after his Father and Mother were killed by Comanches. His brother was six years younger than he was, and was staying with another Aunt at Black Buttes. She was a sister to his Mother, Jane Coulter. His Father, Buck Coulter ran a small ranch out by Turkey Feather Creek, thirty miles from Black Buttes when he was a boy and the Comanches caught his parents out collecting up strays when they attacked them and drove off the cattle. Not knowing what else to do, he saddled up the old mare he rode around the ranch and mounting his little brother behind him, rode over to Franks and Matty's. Frank got some of the other ranch folks and they went and got his Mother and Father in a wagon, taking them to town to be buried there in the Black Buttes graveyard. He was ten years old when it happened and his brother was four. Frank sold the ranch, put what little money there was from the sale in the bank for the two boys and he and his wife raised them like they were their own. Frank and Matty had two sons that died as babys and after the last one Matty almost died. When she got well the Doctor told her she could never have another baby, so they lavished their love on their two nephews. They always had a happy life together on the ranch and now they were gone, shot down by a gang of cut throat outlaws. Harlan thought of these things on his way back home. Home. Not anymore. A month after the raid, he rode into Black Buttes. His Aunt grabbed him in a tearful embrace and his brother was all eyes and questions, for word of his doing reached town before he did.

Sitting in her comfortable kitchen with a cup of strong coffee before him, he told them all what happened. They had not heard from him since the day he left on the trail of the rustlers. He had stopped by and told them about Frank and Matty being killed in the raid, that he buried them and was taking the trail of their killers. He told his Aunt Mary of the money in the bank at Texas Junction and gave her the receipt for it. She told him that a local rancher was interested in buying the ranch so Harlan told her to sell it and use the money for her and his brother for he had unfinished business to take care of. She begged him not to go, to stay and make a life here, but he was determined to find Sam and Jed Clements and make them pay for what they had done!

His Aunt Mary was tall, slim and quite good looking, like his Mother had been. She ran a boarding house offering food and lodging for anyone that needed it. She had been a widow for nearly five years now. Her husband William Bonner was the town Sheriff for several years before he was gunned down in a bank holdup. Four men helt up the bank one morning and he shot it out with them, along with his deputy. They killed them all, but William was so shot up the Doctor could not save him. The deputy recovered from his wounds to became Sheriff after that. Mary swore she would never marry again and never had. She seemed happy running the boarding house and seeing after his brother. Mary had a son about the same age as Harlan, who worked on a nearby ranch, and she had adjusted her life to living as a widow. Harlan finished his coffee, rose and made ready to leave. Telling his brother and his Aunt he would be back when he could, he rode out on the lonely trail of revenge leaving a tearful Aunt and big eyed brother behind.

Many stories were told of Harlan and his long trail. Around campfires and in saloons, anywhere men gathered he was talked about like other men of the gun. Billy the Kid. Earp. Hickok. Ben Thompson and others. He worked at several jobs on his quest. Shotgun guard on the Overland Stage Company. Marshall of a wild cow town. Deputy in another place. Town tamer. Gunman. Cold, fearless, fast with his guns, but he knew when to use a gun and when not to. Men respected and feared him. Some called him their friend, some did not. He was a man apart, searching always. One hot day he caught up with the Clement brothers in a small Texas town called Cottonwood Crossing. Calling them out, he shot both of them and left them lying dead in the hot dusty street. Soon men began to seek him and his fast guns out. Before long he was a bounty hunter, a gun for hire, a man who settled land and cattle disputes. Along the way he picked up the name, "Widow Maker." He was a man of cold nerve having his own code of honor, sometimes serving as Town Marshall of some rough mining town. The pay was good and his wants were few. Once when he was working in Carson City, he met a young lady running a saloon of her own. Her name was Shannon O'donnel and she was beautiful. They took to each other right off and he gave her his protection.

The women in the town wanted her ran out of there because they said no decent woman should run a saloon, but mostly because their husbands liked to drink there. She had a sweet singing voice and the place was packed every night with lonely men including Harlan. They saw a lot of each other and friendship, then, slowly, love blossomed between them. One day the good women of the town decided they would put her on the way attacking the saloon with axe handles and hoes breaking windows and bottles. Harlan came on the run and when he got there, the women were fixing to tar and feather her and run her out of town. He drew one of his Colts, firing a couple of shots at the ceiling. That broke it up, the women running and screaming for safety. Harlan lost his job over it so he and Shannon left town together in a buckboard with their clothes in the rear and his horse tied on behind. They came to another town and Shannon bought another small saloon. Soon her singing packed them in and business was good. Harlan could find no work there so he moved on. They saw each other as much as possible, as Harlan moved around a lot. She was true to him, loving no other man. The mining towns where she worked showered her with gold and she became fairly rich, but still pined for Harlan. He was up in Montana working for a big cattle company there. She knew their paths would cross soon and one night he came riding in to spend a week with her before he left on another big job. They talked of settling down somewhere, buying a ranch and living quietly, but it was all just fond dreams, both knew he would never really get to settle down. His name was too well known. And now, years later they were to meet again. He saw Shannon as often as he could over the years and his brother was serving as Deputy Sheriff in Black Buttes at one time he heard. Harlan was glad he had chosen the law as his profession. After traveling all over the west selling his gun, being in numberless gunfights, here he was now in the town of Twin Rivers. He had kept up with things over the years by listening and asking the right questions. The kettle was about to boil over and he wanted to be here when it did. Already people were beginning to notice him and whisper his name. He settled deeper in his chair, smoked his cigar and took the pulse of the town.

CHAPTER 2

Sheriff Lee Coulter sat behind his desk in the office of the town's jail. His Deputy, Ed Barnes sitting across from him leaned over the desk.

"He is hyar all right Lee. Sittin' over thar in a rocker on the hotel porch big as life. Right hyar in oure town, Harlan Cooper. One uv the fastest gunmen in Texas, an' a lot uv other places. Why do yuh recon he is hyar Lee?"

Ed was an older man who liked to talk, especially about gunmen.

"I don't know Ed, but I am sure we will find out before long."

"Wal I say either Sam Barton er Owen Straight sent fer him, by jacks."

"You could be right Ed. We will just have to wait an' see."

"Anythin' on him in them wanted posters?"

"No, he is not wanted anywhere for anything as far as I can find out. Maybe he is here for another reason all together."

"Maybe. Wal, he has always been a straight shooter. Comes in, does his job, collects his money an' leaves. At least thet is what I have heard."

"The only problem with a known man like Harlan Cooper is that he is a undesirable element and trouble is drawn to him like lightening to a lightening rod. Young guns wanting to make a name for their selfs. A quick reputation. To challenge a man like Harlan is a big thing to some of them anyway. To actually go up against him is something else. He attracts trouble, gun trouble. We don't need that here, especially now."

Ed let his chair down on all four legs. "You ain't gonna try tuh arrest him aire yuh Sheriff?"

Lee let out a long sigh. "I hope it don't come to that Ed."

"Me too," Ed agreed wagging his head, "me too."

Down at the Crystal Palace, Shannon O'donnel heard the news from one of her dancing girls and friend, Sandy Wells.

"Guess who is in town," Sandy remarked to Shannon?

"Who?"

"None other than Harlan Cooper, that's who," Sandy told her with a smile.

Shannon put down the ledger she had been going over, her heart beating a little faster. Harlan. In town! She looked up.

"Harlan is here?" Her green eyes sparkled and a smile tugged at her full red lips.

"Big as life."

"How do you know he is here Sandy?"

"I saw him walking up the street a while ago when I was coming back from the dress makers shop. That's how I know."

"How does he look," Shannon asked in a low voice?

"A little older, but still tall and handsome as always," Sandy laughed.

"Harlan. I met him in Carson City years ago when I was running a saloon and dance hall there. He was the town marshal there, and saved me from a mob that was fixing to tar and feather me, plus run me out of town. I haven't seen Harlan in two years and over. Seems longer. A lot longer."

"How come you too never got married? I know you love each other," Sandy asked?"

"He was always on the move from town to town and I was too. We wanted to marry, but Harlan said he didn't want to make me a widow. In his line of work life was too uncertain he said."

"But look at all the years you have wasted. Years you could have spent together. If I loved, really loved a man, I would not care what he did, I would stay by his side good or bad. One year together would be better than years apart."

Shannon thought about that. "You are right Sandy. We have spent too many years apart. Too many lonely nights. Too many towns behind us. I want to settle down. I want to marry and have children, Harlan's children. We are still young. We could leave here, go someplace where no one knows Harlan Cooper, the Widow Maker. Where men don't have to carry guns, or be afraid of being shot in the back."

Her green eyes glowed as she talked, building castles in the air. Sandy listened, a sad smile on her face.

"I just thought I would let you know he is here Shannon."

But Shannon sat lost in thought. Sandy patted her shoulder and eased out the door, closing it softly behind her.

"Harlan Cooper." Shannon breathed his name. He was the only man she had ever loved, or cared about. She knew who he was and that he could never settle down in any one place. There were too many men who wanted to see him dead. Too many graves behind him. She knew that he cared deeply for her, but could never offer her the things women hold so dear, want and cherish. A home, children, security, someone to grow old with. Harlan would never live to be old, not with his reputation and the life he led. In spite of all that, she would marry him in a minute if he asked her, but there were too many steps on his back trail. She sat like that for some time, her mind in a turmoil, making plans and rejecting them, thinking of what she would say to him when they met again.

We could go away somewhere, a place where people don't know you, she had pleaded the last time they were together. I have money. We could be happy. But he had taken her in his arms and with a sad smile told her that even though he loved her deeply, he had made a promise to someone long ago that kept him from going away. She told him she loved him and that she understood. They saw each other from time to time stealing a few hours away to share their love. Now he had shown up here. That he would seek her out there was no doubt in her mind, for there was a bond between them that being apart could never break.

Harlan sat in his comfortable rocker until late evening. Many were the looks that came his way, some curious, some puzzled. Over the town was a strained quiet. The kind of quiet that comes before a storm. As the sun set in the western sky he rose and stretched, going into the hotel dining room. He took a seat with his back to the wall. The room was noisy, with the clatter of dishes, forks, and people talking. The same cute girl came to his table with a smile on her freckled face bringing him a cup of coffee. He ordered roast beef, mashed potatoes and gravy, with apple pie for desert. He took his time eating, enjoying the good food with the hum like a beehive around him, comming in for his share of glances. The girl kept his cup filled as before as she had done at breakfast. Now she sat a big wedge of pie in front of him, he smiled up at her.

"Apple, that is my favorite."

"I bake them myself," the young lady told him, showing a dimple and white even teeth.

He took a bite. "Umm, that is good."

"My mother showed me how to bake when I was a little girl," she laughed.

He nodded his appreciation as she left to wait on other tables. Getting up, Harlan laid some money on the table for the food, plus a nice tip for the friendly girl. Stepping out on the wide cool porch he lit a cigar and strolled toward the Crystal Palace, his boot heels tapping softly on the wooden boardwalk as he walked along. Darkness had settled over the town and lamps were lit to push back the gloom. Their yellow light shone through windows and out into the street. The Crystal Palace was lit up brightly with light from the hanging chandeliers that gave the place its name. Harlan stopped at the door and looked inside, his eyes probing the interior of the large room. Only after a close look did he venture inside the swinging doors. The sound of a wheel whirling and poker chips clinking caught his ear. The room was full of men bucking the tiger. Several painted girls were scattered around, some of them dancing with the men. A piano, banjo and fiddle provided the music. Men were in off the range craving female companionship of any kind. Shannon's girls were there to dance with the customers and get them to buy drinks only. Any man who wanted more than that had to go to the far end of town to Madame Caroline's gentleman's club for lonely men. She provided a service that was necessary to the town, seeing the men outnumbered the women four to one at least. Harlan's piercing eyes took in the people there in one long sweeping glance, as it was second nature to him. Quickly, silently, he stepped completely inside, his back to the wall, sweeping the room again with his sharp eyes. No one seemed to notice him and that was good, for his life depended on seeing the other man first, a man who might just be waiting for him.

Placing everyone before he reached the bar, he ordered a beer. It was cold and tasted good. He stood at the end of the bar, his back to the wall sipping the beer. There were four tables of card players, seven or eight men around the Roulette wheel, three men at a back table talking and ten or eleven at the bar drinking. Not bad for a week night, but then Twin Rivers was a sizeable town with the two big ranches on either side of it with several smaller ones scattered around. He scanned the crowd for any possible trouble for he knew it could come from any place. Seeing none in the faces there, relaxed, but still aware of everyone, every sound around him. He was like a wolf, circling around, smelling the air for a trap of any kind. He possessed an inner instinct for survival, something born in him that had helped him stay alive over the years. He could react with lightning speed at the first sign of trouble. Only one gun hung at his hip, but there was one under his belt behind him, a short barreled .44 belly gun in a holster under his left arm beneath his leather vest, a .41 double barreled derringer rested in the right side pocket of his vest and a ten inch Bowie knife in his right boot. Harlan always went prepared if trouble reared its ugly head.

There was a lull in the noisy room and he looked toward the broad winding stairway. There she stood at the top of it in a white gown that shimmered in the light, looking like a Princess, her hair done up in long curls with just a touch of makeup. Shannon O'donnel.

The only woman that ever fired his blood. The woman he loved and wanted for his own! He watched her glide down the stairs in regal fashion and make her way to the stage at the far end of the room. All eyes followed her as she crossed the room climbing the three steps onto the stage. The place grew quiet as the small band strummed Beautiful Dreamer.

She sang the song in a soft husky voice, the words floating across the air like a musical fog. Her eyes caught Harlan's across the room and she sang her songs to him as he stood there, a big smile on his face drinking in her beauty. There was not a sound in the room until she finished her song, then the men there burst into a thunderous applause. When the noise quietened down she sang Barbra Allen, and then a haunting ballad about a young Irish Highwayman that hypnotized the crowd. Not a drink was ordered nor a word spoke until her songs were finished, then four pretty young ladies came out on the stage with a rollicking version of Camp Town Races. Shannon left the stage as the crowd roared, throwing money at her feet. She bowed gracefully in the tight gown, smiled and waved at the crowd. Tripping down the steps she came straight toward Harlan. He stood there, tall and silent, the want for her in his eyes plain to see, smelling her perfume as it wafted to him.

She gave him a glad smile. "Buy a girl a drink mister?"

Harlan knew that throaty voice, her green eyes, the bright smile so well. He had dreamed of them when he was on the trail, or trying to stay alive in some new town. Now, here she stood before him, as his eyes devoured her and a happy smile creased his face. She saw the hungry look on his face feeling the same way about seeing him.

"Good to see you Shannon," he said in a hushed voice.

She took his hands in hers. "How long this time Harlan?"

He looked deep into those lovely green eyes. The same eyes that had haunted his dreams, his thoughts on long, hard rides and lonely campfires a lot lately. A smile still tugged at the corners of his mouth.

"If things work out, a long time."

Surprise showed on her face. "You mean you are quitting for good,"? Her voice trembled with emotion as she spoke.

"I am. Just as soon as this last job is over with Shannon."

"That is why you are here, another gun job!"

"Yes. But not like all the others. This time I am keeping a promise I made years ago."

"I remember Harlan," she said as she squeezed his hands.

She came closer; "Let's go up to my rooms so we can talk and not be disturbed."

Shannon led the way across the room and up the stairway to her suite of rooms where she lived. Unlocking the door, she led Harlan inside and turning to him, pressed her lips to his in a warm welcome home kiss. Drawing back she looked into his eyes.

"I am glad you are quitting Harlan, it is time to quit. My God, it is so good to see you again. I have worried about you a lot."

"I know Shannon." His arms tightened around her warm body. "After the promise I made years ago is fulfilled, I am going to hang my guns up for good. No more taming towns, fightin' for other people's land, cattle or mines, I am through. I want to settle down on a ranch somewhere, raise cattle, horses an' kids."

He glanced at her as he said that, seeing her catch her breath and her eyes widen, he laughed.

"Harlan Cooper, are you asking me to marry you?"

"In my own off handed way, I guess I am. Will you?"

"Will I what," she retorted, her eyes flashing.

"Will you marry me?"

"When?"

"As soon as this last job is finished. I don't want to be without you anymore. I want you for my wife."

"Yes," she answered simply.

"Yes what," he asked?

"I will marry you. Today, tomorrow, next week, anytime."

He took her in his arms and lavished all his lonely years on her with kisses. She melted into his arms molding her body to his. When they broke apart, both were panting. He followed her into the bedroom with its big four poster bed. There they removed their clothing and fell upon the soft bed, coming together like they had never been apart. It was nearly daylight when they were finally sated. they fell into a deep peaceful sleep, rising only when the sun was high. Shannon threw the sheets back, looked at Harlan's hard muscled body and crawled on top of him, kissing him fiercely.

Later they sat in her dining room eating ham and eggs that the old cook she employed brought them from the kitchen, along with a pot of coffee along with a plate of biscuits. Both seemed to have a healthy appetite this day. The old cook smiled when she sat the loaded platter on the small table.

"Good to see you again Mr Cooper."

"It is good to see you Jilly an' taste some of your good cookin' again."

She gave him a broad wink. "Will you be needin' anythin' else Miss Shannon?"

"No, this is fine Jilly, thanks."

"All right Mamm. See you young folks later," she laughed.

"That old lady shore can cook," Harlan said.

"Yes she can. She has taught me how over the years too."

"You can cook?"

"I will have you know Harlan Cooper that I am a fine cook. One night before long I shall cook supper for you."

"I would like that Shannon."

Shannon lay down her fork, looking intently across the table at him

'Harlan, go to the hotel and get your things. I want you to move in here with me."

"Do you think that is wise? I could bring trouble to you."

"Nobody would dare come in here starting trouble, the men around would tear them apart."

"All right. I will move my things in here today."

"Good, that settles that," she said leaning across the table giving him a big kiss, a happy smile on her face.

CHAPTER 3

Sheriff Lee Coulter went home to dinner as he did almost every day. The good smell of beef steak, onions and frying potatoes filled the small house as he walked in. His four year old son Wyatt met him as he entered, running across the floor to be scooped up in his Father's arms. Lee swung him around a couple of times, sat him back on the floor then went to kiss his wife's flushed face as she turned from the hot stove.

"Daddy's home," Wyatt announced to his Mother.

"Yes, I can see that he is," she laughed, pulling back from her husband's embrace, to stir the potatoes.

"Is dinner ready hon," Lee asked?"

"By the time you two get washed up it will be. Scoot."

Lee picked up Wyatt carrying him went over to the sink and pumped out some water to wash up in. Wyatt liked splashing in the water, but didn't care much for the soap. Wiping his hands on the towel lying there, declared he was ready to eat. Laughing, Lee picked him up and carried him into the dining room sitting him in a chair at the side of the table, then took his own seat at the head. Wyatt asked him one question after another as they sat there. Sara put the food on the table, poured the coffee, got a glass of milk for Wyatt, then took a seat across from him. Lee cut into his steak with the appetite of a hungry man.

"I heard some news at the store this morning," she remarked.

Her husband looked up at her, his fork poised in the air. "What was that?"

"That there is a gunman in town by the name of Harlan Cooper. Do you know him?"

Lee took his time answering her. "Yes, I know him."

"Is he a real gunman," a big eyed Wyatt asked?"

"Yes son, he is a real dyed in the wool gunman."

"Will you have to shoot him Daddy?"

Lee laughed, "No son, I will not have to shoot him."

His wife sat looking at him, a shadow of fear on her pretty face, and worry in her brown eyes.

"Do you think you will have trouble with him Lee?"

"No," he answered slowly, "not with him."

"How do you know?"

"I know the man. He is not a trouble maker. He is one of the few gunmen who has respect for the law."

"Lew Clark at the store said he has killed fifty men!"

"That would be stretching it a lot I think."

"Will you have to put him in your jail Daddy?"

"No son, I won't have to put him in jail.

"Then what will you do with him Daddy?"

"I think I will just let him alone son."

They finished their dinner in silence, each with different thoughts.

Lee hugged his wife and ruffled his son's hair as he left for the office. Sara watched him stride away down the street, his boots kicking up little puffs of dust. A tall broad shouldered man in Levi's, a red checked shirt and a gray hat. She felt her heart swell with pride at the sight. He was her man and she would fight to keep him safe if need be. Putting Wyatt out in the back yard, she attacked the dirty dishes. Maybe Lee was right. Perhaps there would be no trouble with Harlan Cooper. Still she could not get the thought out of her head. What if Cooper was here to side one of the big ranchers that were squaring off for a range war? Lee had talked to her about it and she knew he was worried over it. Still, it was not right for a wife to stick her nose into her husband's business. But, maybe she could find out why Cooper was in town and let her husband know. The town sat right in the middle of the two big ranches and if a fight broke out it would effect the whole town. Lee and Ed were the only law within a hundred miles or more. Her mind was made up, she would find out why Harlan Cooper was in town if she could!

Back at his office, Lee went through his mail sorting out the different odds and ends. After that walked over to Judge William Hill's office for a talk with the wiley old man. He opened the door. Judge Hill looked up from his work, waving him in.

"Evening Judge."

"Good afternoon Lee, have a seat. You look like a man with something on his mind that needs to be discussed with an old friend."

"You read me right sir, I do," Lee sighed as he began to talk about the tension building up around the town. Judge Hill puffed on a fat cigar as he listened, nodding from time to time.

"You see a range war coming, don't you son."

"Yessir I do. It will split this town wide open. Men will be picking sides in it and if it don't rain soon, blood will wet the ground I am afraid. Barton's fork of the river is getting lower and he is pawing the ground like one of his bulls."

"Yes, he can be hot headed at times," the Judge agreed, "but so can Straight. Two hard headed men can be like a keg of gunpowder, one hot spark can set them off."

"Well, neither one of them will give an inch, and you know what that means Judge, gun trouble. Both of them have fifteen men or so riding for them. Can you imagine what they would do to this town if a fight breaks out? I think the fight will be fought here Judge, not out on the range because each of them believe the town will side them!

"I think you are right Lee. The number of men on either side will decide the outcome of a fight, and if both of them believe that the town will side them, they will bring the fight here. You are correct on that Lee."

Lee turned his hat in his strong hands. "I just hope I am wrong this time."

Judge Hill sat back in his chair and peered at Lee over his glasses, "this Harlan Cooper who came to town, do you think he is here to hire his gun out to Barton or Straight?"

Lee gave him a straight look. "I wish I knew Judge. It would make my job a lot easier, that is for sure."

"So, you have no idea why he is here in Twin Rivers?"

Lee studied for a minute. "Maybe, I don't know Judge. I will go have a talk with him. Maybe if I explain things to him, he might understand what a bad position the town is in."

"Are you going to warn him out of town son?"

"No sir, just have a man to man talk with him. I don't know if he will tell me anything, but I can try."

"Well, you know your business Sheriff."

Lee stood up to leave. "I will keep you informed Judge."

"Do that. And say hello to your wife for me."

Lee nodded to the Judge, set his Stetson square on his head and left.

Out in the street, he looked up and down, noticing there were less people on the streets than usual, his gaze centering in on the hotel porch where Harlan sat most of the time, but he wasn't there today. Lee strolled up that way at a slow walk. The porch was empty of chair polishers today for some reason. He walked into the lobby only to find two drummers talking and an old white bearded fellow reading a faded newspaper. A thought crossed his mind, and he went back outside wending his steps toward the Crystal Palace. Going into the big cool room, he crossed the floor to the polished bar. The bartender turned from where he was washing glasses.

"Howdy Sheriff."

"Evening Henry."

"Something I can do for you?"

"Have you seen anything of a man called Harlan Cooper?"

The bartender nodded. "There he comes down the stairs now Sheriff."

Lee turned to look. Harlan came walking toward him, a slight smile on his clean shaven face. "Looking for me Sheriff," he asked in a soft drawl?

Lee nodded. "Got time for a pow wow?"

Harlan pointed to a table in the back corner. "How about over there Lee."

The Sheriff followed him over to the round table with its six chairs, and noticed that Harlan took a seat so he could face the whole room. He sat down across from him and removed his hat. Harlan studied him for a minute, then nodded as if satisfied with what he saw.

"You look good Lee, but I guess you are wondering what I am doin' here."

"The thought did cross my mind Harlan."

"Not what you are thinkin'. This town is gettin' ready to be swallowed up in a fight over water. That is why I am here."

"Your gun record follows you wherever you go Harlan."

"I know that, but this time it is not for sale at any price to either side!"

"Then why are you here?"

Shannon came gliding down the broad stairs then and Harlan inclined his head toward her. "There is part of the reason."

Lee nodded as he glanced at her. "O K, what is the other reason?"

Harlan sat holding his eyes for several seconds before replying.

"You will find out when the times comes, but I will promise you this, I am not here to sell my gun, or cause you any kind of trouble, if anything, I might be able to save you some trouble Lee."

"And how is that?"

"Give me a Deputy's badge an' let me work for you!"

The flat statement hit Lee like a load of bricks. "You want to be my Deputy? Is this a joke? No, wait, you are serious about it, am I right?"

"I was never more serious in my life Lee."

"I know you have worn the badge a few times before, but why here and why now?"

"I only want the job until this trouble is settled, then I am going to quit an' hang up my guns for good. In the short time I have been here, I have spotted three new hired guns. Money an' a fight draws them like honey draws a bear. This range will bust wide open in a few more days an' you could use a man like me on your side."

Lee looked thoughtful. The idea appealed to him, but slowly he shook his head.

"I wish I could Harlan, but the town council would crucify me if I did."

Harlan grinned and shrugged his shoulders. "Just remember Lee, I will be here if you need me, an' I will back you till Hell freezes over!"

"What you said about quitting and hanging up your guns Harlan, you really mean it?"

"I do. I have even asked Shannon to marry me too, an' she said yes."

Lee smiled. "I am glad for you Harlan, I really am. You deserve some happiness."

He rose from his chair, "I will remember what you said, but that is just between us."

Harlan got up from his chair to meet the Sheriff's outstretched hand in a firm grip. Their eyes locked, and a smile crossed Lee's face.

"For what it is worth Harlan, it is good to see you. You look well."

"I am Lee. The decision has been made, an' I am stickin' to it."

Getting to the swinging doors, Lee glanced back to see Harlan watching him. He was a man at ease in any surroundings. Lee was in his surroundings but he was not a man at ease by any standard.

CHAPTER 4

That night when her show was over, Shannon and Harlan went upstairs to her rooms. Inside she threw herself into his arms and he drew her close, kissing her full red lips, her eyes, her throat, her soft neck and shoulders as she clung to him in a desperate embrace, her eyes shut, giving him back kiss for kiss.

"Why did you stay away from me so long," she whispered?"

"We will never be apart again, I promise you that."

"No, we won't. We are together now for always."

He packed her to a chair and sat down with her on his lap.

"When this trouble is over, we will go away some where far from here, where nobody knows me."

"Oh Harlan, how I have hoped and prayed for this. All those years of moving from town to town, never knowing if you were alive or dead. You are here with me now and it will be like it was in Silver City that time."

"I remember that well. The happiest time of my life."

"It will be even better now."

"I have cherished every moment I ever spent with you Shannon."

He could see the love shining in her smoky green eyes, as she snuggled deeper into his embrace. Arm in arm, they made their way into the bedroom.   Next morning Harlan went to his hotel room and brought all his belongings over to Shannon's room. He had just finished doing that when the Sheriff came in to see him. After Lee left, he was still sitting at the table working with a deck of cards to help keep his fingers limber when the doors swung inward and three men came stomping in like they owned the place. The foremost was a beefy red faced man with an arrogant expression on his unsmiling face. He looked around, saw Harlan sitting there and came over towards him. He stepped up to where he sat at the table, the other two trailing him.

"Yuh Harlan Cooper," he asked in a loud authoritative voice!

Harlan looked up coldly. "Who wants to know?"

"My name is Owen Straight. I own the Bar O. Like tuh talk tuh yuh."

Without waiting for an answer, he pulled out a chair and sat down.

"This valley is gittin' ready tuh bust wide open Cooper. I control all the land East uv Twin Rivers. Sam Barton has the West side an' Barton is tryin' tuh push me off my land. I won't stand fer it. I want yuh tuh ramrod my crew. They aire salty 'nuff an' with a top gun tuh lead 'em, we kin cut Barton off at the knees."

Harlan sat quietly, just staring at the man. He shook his head. "No."

"Whut?"

"I said no Straight, I am not interested."

"Why?"

"I am not lookin' for a job."

"Already got one huh. Maybe yuh done hired out yore gun tuh Barton!"

"No, I am not workin' for Barton or you either Straight."

Straight's face got even redder at the flat statement.

"I will pay yuh top wages. Two hunerd a month an' keep."

Harlan's gray eyes were hard and cold as he looked at the man. "The answer is still no!"

Straight stood up so quick he turned over his chair, his big hairy fists balled into hard knots.

"You may not work fer me Cooper, but by Gawd I will see tuh it yuh don't work fer Barton either!"

Harlan looked at him through unsmiling, deadly eyes, his mouth a tight thin line pinning Straight where he stood.

"Our talk is over Straight," he told him in a mild voice, "now get out of my face an' take your bootlickers with you. Now!"

One of the other men, a raw boned young tough with long scraggley blonde hair, a Colt .45 hanging on his hip stepped back, his hand sliding down towards his gun.

"He don't look so tough tuh me Mr Straight," he snarled.

Harland stared at him with a frosty smile. "Feel lucky today boy?'

"Git tuh yore hoss Luke," Straight ordered. "When the time comes, Cooper will git his in spades!"

Luke threw Harlan an evil grin as he turned to leave. Straight stood staring at Harlan with a dark scowl on his face, then he turned on his heel and stomped back out of the saloon, the other man following him as he slammed through the swinging doors.

Harlan let out a deep sigh. It was happening all over again. There was always someone wanting to hire his fast gun. His guns were not for hire this time and not in this town.

CHAPTER 5

Later that evening, Harlan sat with Shannon having supper in her dining room. She smiled across the table at him.

"So, you turned Owen Straight down flat."

He laughed, "yes, an' it felt good too."

"You really mean it this time, you are going to put away your guns for good, marry me and settle down," she said, her green eyes flashing.

"Yes I do. I want to hang up my guns an' settle down with you. Raise some cattle an' horses along with a few kids."

"How many is a few?"

"Oh, five or six."

She threw back her head and laughed. "You talk like you are going to make a brood mare out of me after we are married Harlan."

He laughed along with her. "I do want children though."

"So do I, I love babies. It all sounds good to me Harlan and I like that part about kids.

He leaned over the table. "It will be good to have a home again after all these years."

She took his hands. "So far it has just been a dream, but we can make it come true, I know we can. I have money saved and this place will bring a good price."

"I have some money saved too," Harlan mused, "between us I think we can swing a ranch somewhere, an' stock it."

Shannon's face was glowing as they talked about their future and laid plans. They sat talking the evening away about all the things they planned to do. All too soon it was time for her to go to work and sing to the crowd. The patrons looked forward to her singing every night. They walked down the stairs together, out onto the saloon floor. Shannon made her way to the stage and Harlan took his usual seat in the corner. He was carrying two Colt .44's, plus a derringer was tucked in his vest pocket. Harlan looked slimmer than his one ninety, and most people guessed him ten pounds lighter, but he looked bigger with his guns on. t

Shannon was on her next song when hatchet face man with a scar someone in his past had taken a swipe at him with a knife walked up to his table. He was rawboned and looked like he was made out of bobwire and saddle leather. His voice had a twangy sound as he introduced himself.

"Howdy, my name is Sam Barton. Hev a ranch West uv hyar. Aire yuh Harlan Cooper?"

Harlan nodded.

"Wal Mr Cooper, I want tuh hire yuh."

"My gun is not for hire Barton," Harlan told him in no uncertain terms.

Barton helt up a big paw. "Hear me out. I will pay two hunnerd a month an' found, plus a thousand dollars bonus when Straight's hash is settled."

"I repeat, my guns are not for hire."

"Yore makin' a big mistake gunhand. I hev eighteen men ridin
fer me, an' they would tear yuh apart if I give 'em the word!

"Well Barton, if you come against me, you will need every one
of them!"

Barton snorted. "Bah. All yuh fancy gunslingers aire jist alike.
Take away yore guns, an' you ain't nuthin!"

"You want to try takin' them," the icy voice asked?"

Sam Barton laid both big weathered hands on the table and
leaned forward.

"I hev buried many a man who crossed me. If yuh sell yore
gun's tuh Straight, dont git in my way, fer I will plow yuh under!"

With a final glare from his cold blue eyes, he turned and left.

Harlan watched him leave, a crooked smile on his face. When
Shannon finished her set she made her way to his table. He stood to
greet her and pulled out a chair beside him.

"Another job offer," she asked, sitting down in the chair he
was holding for her.

"Yes. It seems like my services are in demand," he grimaced.

"What is this business you have in town Harlan and how soon
will it be finished?"

"I cannot tell you the true nature of it, an' I do not know when
it will be finished. But I can promise you this, as soon as it is over, we
are gettin' married an' leaving town."

"What is to stop us from getting married now, tomorrow
morning Harlan?"

"Why nothing really, but I had rather wait."

"I think we have waited long enough, too long in fact. Look at
the time we have already lost not being together. You were always
afraid you might leave me a widow, but look my darling, in the past
five years we have not spent much time together on account of that. I
don't want to lose another day, I want to be your wife now. I don't
want to spend any more time worrying about what might happen.
Let's live for today and not worry about what tomorrow might bring."

There were unshed tears in her eyes and Harlan took her soft
hands in his nodding his head.

"You are right Shannon, we have wasted too much time. Being apart when we could have been together living as man an' wife. All right, I will go see the preacher in the morning an' get the ball rolling."

At one o'clock next day, Harlan and Shannon were married in the little white church at the end of town. It was a small service with Sandy as bridesmaid and the bartender as best man. Word soon spread around town of the wedding. That night a wedding party was helt in the Crystal Palace and the place was packed. Shannon floated around the room in a long white dress that showed off all her well rounded figure. Harlan looked fit and trim in a new dark suit and polished boots. It was his wedding night, but he carried two Colts, also a Derringer out of sight. The drinks flowed like water, as a happy crowd toasted the bride and groom over and over. Finally at eleven o'clock, Harlan and Shannon slipped off to her quarters upstairs. Once inside with the doors locked, Harlan took off his coat laying the pistols nearby. He opened a magnum of champagne, and they sat sipping the bubbly liquid as Shannon kept looking at the rings on her finger.

She smiled at Harlan, "I can hardly believe we are married. After all the years of different towns and being apart so much."

"You heard the preacher, for better or worse, till death do we part," Harlan quipped.

"We have had the worst so far, now comes the better. The part about death will just have to come much later my dear," she told him.

Finishing her drink, she stood and began to take off her dress. "Unbutton me darling."

Harlan sat down his glass, and stood behind her, slipping the buttons through the holes. In a few minutes she stood naked before him and Harlan marveled at her beauty. He undressed quickly. Sweeping her up in his strong arms, he carried her into the bedroom. He lay her on the big four poster bed join her there. They made love for the first time as man and wife with Shannon clinging to him as if she would never let him go.

The next day passed by peacefully for the town, but on the following day, two new faces showed up. They tied their horses in front of the Crystal Palace, and after a long look up and down the street, walked in, spurs jingling, their pistols tied down. Harlan was sitting at his usual table shuffling cards and drinking a cup of coffee when they strolled in. He knew them on sight. Stud Walters and his partner, Tico Jones, a couple of pistoleros and back shooters. They had ridden together for years selling their guns out to the highest bidder. No job was too rough for them, and they worked like wolfs on a trail. Ambush was one of their favorite tricks, for they always wanted an edge. They got the job done and didn't care how they did it. All was fair to them in their style of fighting.

Leaning against the bar, drinks in hand, they let their eyes roam over the room. Harland came under the searching eyes, but with his hat pulled low over his brow, his face was in the shadows. Their eyes roamed the room and moved on past him, but Stud's gaze came back to him a couple of times as though there was something familiar about him. Something about that still figure tugged at his memory. Harlan allowed himself a tight smile. A few years ago, he had backed Stud down in a small cantina near the border, took his gun away from him and slapped his ears down in front of a crowd. He knew that Stud would always hate him for that.

"Hey bartender," Tico called, "can you tell us how to get to the Box B?"

The bartender looked up from polishing glasses and told him, "ride due west, an' you will come to it after about three miles."

Stud and Tico finished their drinks, flipped a coin on the bar and left. As he got to the swinging doors, Stud turned to take another look at the still figure sitting at the corner table. There was something about the man that bothered Stud, but he couldn't put his finger on it.

Harlan sat and watched them leave. The Buzzards were gathering and Lee would have to be on his guard from now on. As he sat there deep in thought, shuffling the cards, Shannon came over and sat down with him.

"Those two men just in here, did you know them Harlan?"

"Yes, I knew them. Guns for hire."

"Harlan, I am beginning to get scared. This town is running scared. This morning at the store, men in there were talking of taking side if it comes to a fight."

"How will they go?"

"They were split about even. Some want to close up their business's and get away, but there is no place for them to go. Do you think the fight will be here, in town?"

"I believe it will. They will want to get rid of the Sheriff an' his Deputy first, then they will have the town bluffed. To kill them, they shall have to come here. The Sheriff is a good man an' needs all the help he can get."

Shannon stared at him out of wide eyes. "That is why you are here," she whispered, "to help the Sheriff!"

"Yes, that is one reason for my being here. I heard of this oncoming fight over water rights an' I came to offer my help an' my guns. But he is not the only reason I came here, I also came to see you, to make you my wife."

"But why should you help the Sheriff Harlan, take a chance on being killed now that we are together and married now? Why?"

He looked at her with sad eyes. "Because he is my brother."

"Your brother? Lee is your brother?"

"Yes. No one knows that but me an' him. Now you know too. I ask you to keep my secret."

She looked at him through tear dimmed eyes. "Oh Harlan, the promise you made years ago, it was to him wasn't it?"

"It was. I promised to help him if ever he needed me. He was only four when our parents died. Our Aunt an' Uncle raised us. The day I rode out on this long trail I have followed, I made him that promise an' I mean to keep it."

"But how did you know where to find him after all those years?"

"I have kept up with him an' his career through other people. I also knew you were here too Shannon. I had to come."

"I am so glad you did my darling and I will keep your secret. Come, let's go upstairs where we can be alone."

They rose and went up the stairway, Shannon's arm linked through his.

CHAPTER 6

In two days, Harlan counted five gun hands he knew ride through town. He decided it was time to have a talk with the Sheriff. He told Shannon where he was going, and stepped out onto the plank walk. It was a short walk to the Sheriff's office and Lee looked up as he entered.

"Harlan. Have a seat."

Taking a chair across from the Sheriff, Harlan slid his hat back on his head.

Lee grinned at him, shaking his hand across the desk, "Congratulations on getting married. She is a beautiful lady."

Harlan grinned back. "Thanks. I should have done it long ago."

"What brings you by," Lee asked as he leaned back in his chair?

"We need to have a long talk about the situation here. Have you noticed any strange riders comin' into town the past few days?"

"Now that you mention it, I have."

"All top gunhands Lee, rough an' ready to fight. Guns for hire."

"I heard you have had a couple of offers yourself Harlan."

"Yeah. Told them I was not interested an' they got mad about it."

"You know any of these gunhands that have drifted in?"

"I know them all Lee. Stud Walters, his partner Tico Jones, Jim Slade, Chet Brown, an' a kill crazy little fellar that calls hisself Kid Cody."

"I am thinking about posting notices in town forbidding the wearing of guns in the city limits."

"That won't work with these boys Lee, they will make you enforce it to the limit. They respect only one thing, a faster gun. When you go out on the street, always take a double barreled Express shotgun loaded with double ought. They also respect one of them an' it will get their attention where nothin' else would."

"When you speak of a faster gun, you mean yourself."

"I do. Them boys know me, an' that it has been my trade for years."

"What do you think will happen Harlan?"

"There will be a few fights here in town, gunplay out on the range, things like that. That is meant to lure you out of town an' if they can do that, they will kill you Lee."

"You think it has gotten that bad?"

"I have seen it happen before. Barton an' Straight know that you are the only law around for miles. If they can get rid of you, they will have the town bluffed. No one here will send for outside help. Then Barton and Straight will go for each other an' to hell with the town. Winner take all. If they can't lure you out of town, they will set you up here on the street. One of the gunhawks will pick a fight with you, an' trap you into a cross fire!"

Lee looked very thoughtful. Images of his wife and son passed through his mind. What would they do if something happened to him?"

"What you say makes sense Harlan, but I am the Sheriff here. I can't run or hide."

"They know that Lee, an' that is your weakness. What about the city council, the rest of the towns people, will they back you?"

"They are merchants, shopkeepers and the like. None of them would be willing to stand up to a crowd of gunmen. They want to wait and let things work their way out. Not get involved in it. They say it is my job to take care of it. The town's people are not going to cut their own throats by going against the big ranchers. Between them, Barton and Straight have enough men to burn this town to the ground and the people know it. They are afraid. Most of them have families to think of."

"So do you," Harlan said softly.

Lee nodded at that, a forlorn expression in his eyes, then he said, "But this is my job Harlan. The people in this town depend on me for protection!"

"You need help Lee, an' I am the man for the job!"

"I can't, you know that."

"I know how to handle these kind of men. They know me, an' that I will shoot, an' shoot to kill!"

"You don't think I can handle this?"

"Only up to a point. You have never faced men like these. You have to be tougher than them. Meaner, faster with a gun, ready to shoot, no fair breaks. They are a different breed of men than you have ever faced before. I know that you are a brave man Lee, but these men you are going to face up to will eat you alive, for the simple reason that you are a fair, honest, decent man with honor. All the quality's they do not possess. That will stand against you in a fight like the one comin' Lee. I know. I have lived through them."

"I don't know Harlan. I would like to deputize you, but...."

"Is there a telegraph in town?"

"No. The line hasn't gotten here yet."

"Then you can't send for help."

"No. Only by mail. The freight wagons that carry the goods in here carry the mail in an' out."

"When are they due again?"

"Almost two weeks. They run through here every month."

Harlan seemed thoughtful as he looked across the desk at his younger brother.

"Maybe I could swear in a few more deputy's," Lee said.

"Even if you could get a few more men, the hired guns would either shoot them, or back them down. That would make the situation worse. No, what you need is a man who will meet then on their own ground!"

Just then Deputy Ed Barnes came into the office; "Sheriff, a rider jist come intuh town an' tol me there had been a shootin' out at the Bar O. Two strange men shot one uv the cowboys thar an' the cook. Killed the cowboy an' said the cook wuz jist winged. Straight wants yuh out thar pronto!"

Lee threw Harlan a sharp look.

Harlan nodded, "it has started already."

Getting to his feet, Lee strapped on his gun belt, and looked over at Harlan, "I have to go, it's my job!"

Harlan got up out of his chair, "I am goin' with you Lee."

The Sheriff nodded. "All right. Ed, get the horses."

Ed threw the two men a puzzled glance, and shrugging his shoulders, hurried out the door towards the livery stable. Harlan crossed the street going into the Crystal Palace and up the stairs to the rooms he shared with Shannon. She sat at her desk working on her ledger and bills for the month and looked up as he entered knowing something had happened when she saw his face.

"What's wrong Harlan?"

"There has been a shootin' out at the bar O. One of Straight's riders was killed, an' the cook wounded!"

"So, it has started already."

"It seems like it Shannon. I am goin' out there with the Sheriff an' his deputy."

She rose and put her arms around him and a faint smell of perfume touched his nostrils. "Please be careful my love."

"I will, I promise."

"I don't think I could stand it if something were to happen to you now Harlan."

He kissed her trembling lips. "Don't worry over me my lovely wife, I bear a charmed life with your love to protect me."

She laughed in spite of herself. "Go. Go before I lose my nerve and beg you to stay."

He kissed her again, grabbed up his rifle and went out the door. When he came back to the Sheriff's office, he was wearing both Colts along with the Winchester .44-40 in his left hand. Ed came up leading the horses and mounting up, they headed east out of town. Many eyes followed them as they rode out wondering what was going on and why a known gunman like Harlan Cooper was riding with the Sheriff. One pair of eyes that watched them leave were green and full of tears.

They rode into the Bar O ranch yard to find Owen Straight and some of his men standing in front of the bunk house. Dismounting Lee looked at Straight.

"What happen here Owen?"

"Bushwackers, thet's what," was the flat answer. "Two gunnies rode in hyar, an' ketchin Shorty an' Sourdough alone started shootin' at 'em. Killed Shorty an' jist winged Sourdough, an' then they rode off like their britches wuz on fire hollarin' like they wuz crazy!"

"Know who they were Owen?"

"Nope. But Sourdough said one uv 'em yelled out somethin' about it being a message frum Barton! Tuh git out er git buried!"

Sitting his saddle as Lee and Straight talked, Harlan saw two men he knew from years ago. He had seen them when they rode through town. Fast guns for hire. They studied him and wondered what he was doing riding with the Sheriff. Rolling a slim cigar between his lips, Harlan sized them up. Jim Slade and Brown Hardin would fight at the drop of a hat and fight to the last drop of blood in them. But they did not fight for the fun of it, only money. Gun wages. Harlan knew neither of them were flash in the pan gunslingers, but true warriors. Not back shooters like Stud and Tico. They would give you a chance, and it would be face to face. There was a code of ethics among the real gunfighters, not like the dregs of the so called gunmen, backshooters, ambushers, there was no code of ethics among them, no honor, just to kill a man any way you could. Harlan saw quite a few over the years, but Jim and Brown had never stooped that low to earn a dollar, and Harlan knew they never would. They were gunfighters in the true sense of the word, to face your man to depend on the speed in your arm, the trueness in your aim to outdraw him and shoot him before being shot. That was the rule they lived by.

When Lee finished his talk with Straight, he climbed back into the saddle and swung his horse around. Harlan touched his hat in a salute to Jim and Brown. They nodded to him as he rode by them.

Back at the Sheriff's office, Lee filled Harlan and Ed in on the conversation with Straight.

"He wants me to arrest Barton for the shootin' of his men."

"Thet would be jist plain suacide Lee," Ed spoke up shaking his head.

Lee glanced over at Harlan, "what do you think?"

"I agree with Ed. Goin' out there an' tryin' to arrest Sam Barton would be a bad mistake. You would be playin' right into his hands. If the two gunnies that done the shootin' out at Straights do work for him, you comin' out there would be all the reason they need to ambush you when you leave. Instead of you goin' out there, have Barton come in to see you."

Lee studied for a minute, then nodded his head. "That might work even better."

"Barton will come in, if only to deny any knowledge of the shootin' and of the men who did it. His comin' in will show you how well he cooperates with the law."

The Sheriff wrote out a brief note, handing it to Ed. "Take this out to Barton. He won't see you as a threat to him as he would me."

Ed looked a little doubt-full, but then giving the Sheriff a nod, left the office and rode off West out of town.

"A good man there Lee."

"Yes he is. Ed has a little age on him, but he is steady and dependable.

The Sheriff lit a slim cigar and looked over his desk at the man across from him. "You have done this sort of thing before, haven't you?"

Harlan pushed back his hat. "The times that I have worn the badge, I learned a lot of tricks. Some people will show one side to the law, while the other side is hatchin' up a scheme of some sorts. I have been in several range wars on both sides of the badge, as either a hired lawman or a hired gun. But I have never done anything that I was ashamed off."

Lee gave him a long look. "I believe you Harlan."

They studied each other for the space of several heart beats. Gray eyes locked on gray eyes. Sheriff of a western town miles from another settlement and one of the deadliest gunmen in the west.

"What really brought you here Harlan?"

"I think you know Lee."

"Yes," Sheriff Coulter nodded, "I guess I do at that."

"I never break a promise, never."

"What are you and Shannon going to do after this feud is over?"

"I am going to hang my guns up an' take her away somewhere where a man does not need to carry a gun, or where anyone knows of me. A place where I will not have to keep looking over my shoulder. She is a beautiful woman. I love her an' she loves me."

Lee's face wore a happy expression. "I am glad Harlan, glad for the both of you."

They sat in silence smoking, each with his own thoughts. The only sound in the room was the ticking of the clock as time drug by. A horse loping down the street caught their attention. It stopped outside, there was the creak of a saddle, the door opened and Ed came in.

"Barton said tuh tell yuh he would be hyar at nine oclock in the mawnin' Sheriff."

"Thanks Ed. Did he say anythin' else?"

"No. Jist that he would be hyar in the mawnin', an' grinned when he said it."

The Deputy sat in a vacant chair and fired up his old stubby pipe. Harlan rose to leave, stretching his arms over his head.

"See you two in the mornin'"

Lee waved a hand and Ed nodded from behind a cloud of pipe smoke.

Harlan went through the saloon climbing up the stairs to his and Shannon's rooms. He found her still sitting with the accounts book. Crossing over to her, he bent to kiss her neck but she turned quickly presenting her lips instead. He drew back from those full red lips, his hands on her shoulders.

"I watched you ride out with the Sheriff and Deputy," she said quietly, her green eyes searching his gray ones. "How were things out at Straight's place?"

"He was mad. Wanted Barton arrested."

"Is the Sheriff going to arrest him?"

"No. There is no evidence pointin' to him."

"Why did you ride out there Harlan?"

"I wanted to look things over. Saw a couple old gunslingers out there we both know."

"Who was that?"

"Jim Slade an' Brown Hardin. Remember them?"

"Yes I do. They used to come into my place in Silver City a lot. I liked them. They were polite men, and quiet, never caused any trouble at all. Just drank and gambled. They did not look like the bad gunmen they were said to be."

"For gunslingers, they are not bad men at all. At least they face their victims."

"Is the Sheriff going to offer you a job?"

Harlan shook his head. "No, he can't because of the city council."

"But he would like to though."

He needs me Shannon. This bunch will swallow him whole."

"You are willing to stand beside him even though both of you might be killed."

"I must Shannon."

She put her arms around him and he drew her down into his lap as he sat back in a chair. "I know, the promise you made."

"Come and let me tell you a story I have never told anyone."

Sitting on his lap, her arms around him she listened as he told her of two Orphans and their struggle to become men. She listened with tears in her eyes, her head on his shoulder. When he was finished she kissed him, a long deep kiss full of emotions and understanding.

"I am glad you told me your story Harlan. I never knew that before. Now I understand better about everything," she whispered. "You will have all my love and support to help you through this my darling as you support and help your brother."

Harlan gathered her in his arms, holding her as a drowning man might grasp something thrown to him in deep water.

CHAPTER 7

Next morning at eight thirty, Harlan entered the Sheriff's office, a brace of Colt .44's strapped at his waist. Lee sat behind his desk, a double barreled Express shotgun leaning against it near his hand. He glanced up as Harlan entered.

"Morning Harlan."

"Get any sleep last night Lee?"

"Not much. I had a lot on my mind."

"Well, it won't be long now," Harlan remarked, glancing at the clock.

"No, it won't be," Lee said looking out the barred window at the dusty street in front of his office.

Ed came in and took a seat behind and to one side of the Sheriff, and Harlan found a chair in the dark corner by the cells. The clock ticked off the minutes slowly as they sat there in silence. There came the sound of hard ridden horses out upon the street as three riders drew up in front of the office. They tied up their horses, opened the door to came in stomping inside. Sam Barton, with his fierce look and stalking presence was first, followed by two of his riders. He stared at the Sheriff with hard eyes shining in his scowling face.

"Yuh wanted tuh see me!"

It was more of a challenge than a question, the words tipped in poison.

"Yes I do. Have a seat."

Barton sat down in a chair in front of the desk facing Lee. His two riders stood against the wall, smoking, sardonic mocking grins on their faces as they stared at the Sheriff.

Lee got right to it; "I had a call to come out to Owen Straight's ranch yesterday," and he stated the case as Barton glared at him out of his cold blue eyes, a sneer on his face showing his yellow, wolfish teeth.

"I wuz out tuh my ranch all day yestiddy an' so wuz my riders. We moved cattle around on the range gittin' ready fer brandin'."

The two riders nodded agreement with their boss. "Thet's rite," one of them said, "we wuz all out there except the cook, an' he is too fat an' lazy tuh ride any wheres."

They laughed at the statement and their idea of a joke.

"No one knew the men who did the shooting, so I know it wasn't any of your regular hands."

"So, you got nothing on me 'cept the ramblin's uv Straight. Jist because we aire havin' trouble over water, he thinks it wuz me behind the shootin". Barton leaned back in his chair and laughed.

"These were hired guns. Strangers to Straight's men."

Barton snorted his disgust.

"There have been several gun hands drifting into town the past few days."

Lee leaned across his desk, his gray eyes boring into Barton's.

"So whut?"

"How many do you have on your payroll?" The question was like a shot.

Barton's pale blue eyes narrowed as his nostrils flared. "Aire yuh accusin' me uv hirin' gunslingers an' sending them out to shoot up Straight's place?"

Lee laid both hands flat on his desk. "Did you?"

Barton jumped up, kicking his chair backwards in his fury. "If thar wuz fightin' out thar 'er not, yore crossin' the line with me Coulter, acuzin' me uv sendin' hired gunmen out thar", the words spoken in a chilling voice!

Lee stood to face him across the desk. "Don't threaten me Barton," he told him in a cold flat voice, "I am the law here. It is my job to get to the bottom of the killing out at Straights ranch!"

"Not fer long," Barton hissed, "yuh aire cuttin' too big a swath with thet badge!"

He spun on his heel to leave, followed by his grinning riders. At the door he paused for a parting shot.

"Don't git in my way Sheriff, er yuh jist might git trampled underfoot!"

The door slammed, and he was gone with the thunder of hooves on the hard packed street. Harlan came out of the dark corner where he had been listening.

"There goes one angry dangerous man," he said.

Lee nodded his head agreeing with him.

That night, riders from the Box B and the Bar O filled the town. There was drinking and fighting all up and down the street. Before the night was over gunfire filled the air. Two Bar O hands were wounded, and one of the Box B punchers was killed. Lee, Ed and the doctor had a busy night. The air in Twin Rivers was charged with an undercurrent of violence. The whole town was on edge. Doors were locked and shades were drawn. It was daylight when the streets were finally cleared, and the last cow puncher rode out of town, except for the three locked up in jail. Next morning bright and early, the Mayor and the four council members were in Lee's office. He sat at his desk after a long sleepless night, drinking strong black coffee filling out a report on last night's mayhem. The Mayor, Judd Minor did the talking for them.

"Sheriff, something must be done about this violence. We do not want a repeat of last night in our fair town. Have you arrested the man who killed the Box B cowboy? We cannot have this fighting in the streets. Some innocent person could get killed. What have you done so far to stop this?"

The Mayor stood with his hands gripping his coat lapels, as though he was making a speech to get re-elected rambling on and on. Lee sat and listened until he ran out of steam.

"I have three men locked up, but I do not know if one of them is the killer. Judge Hill will set a court date today, and we will get to the bottom of it. We may never find the shooter, but, I will do my best. The only way to stop the shooting in the streets is for the city council to pass a ordinance forbidding the wearing of guns in the city limits, and I will enforce it. But, and this is a fact. I need more men, or at least one good man who knows his business and has done this before."

"This kind of thing must be stopped Sheriff. We cannot have our citizens going around scared for their lives!"

"Do you want me to swear in a couple of Deputy's Mayor? How about two of you?"

The Mayor drew back at the question. He looked at the floor, then back up at Lee. "We are not men of violence Sheriff. We do not carry guns. We are just business men, not lawmen. You are our Sheriff. We leave the guns and keeping of the law up to you. And, the hiring of one deputy only for the present."

Lee nodded. "I understand Judd that hiring three or four deputy's would only upset the town more. What I need is a man, one good man who can meet them on their own grounds. A man with courage who knows when to shoot and when not to. A man who is not afraid of them, and will stand up to them and back my every play. Someone who has had experience handling this sort of thing!"

"Do you know of such a man Sheriff?"

"I do. He is in town now."

"Who is this man Lee?"

"Harlan Cooper!"

The name hung in the air as the Mayor stared at him, dumbfounded.

"Harlan Cooper! The notorious gunfighter? The one they call "Widow Maker"?

"The very same."

"But, the man is a killer. A hired gunman!"

"Harlan is not a killer in the sense you mean Mayor. He has killed men over the years, but he is not blood thirsty. He has always shot men face to face and they all had their chance. He has his own code of honor about him and besides that, Harlan has worn the badge in several tough towns. He knows the law."

The flustered Mayor looked at the council members. They looked at him, then at each other, and reluctantly gave their consent.

"All right Sheriff," the Mayor nodded, a frown on his face, "hire him, but, only until this dispute between Straight and Barton is settled," he sighed.

Lee send Ed over to the Crystal Palace to tell Harlan of the council's decision on hiring him. In a few minutes Harlan stood in the Sheriff's office being sworn in. He smiled as Lee pinned the badge on him.

"I hope this is not a mistake," Lee said as he stepped back.

"It's not," Harlan replied, "any orders for the day?"

"Just keep your eyes and ears open, you and Ed."

Lee shook his hand as he left his office.

Word of the new deputy soon spread around town like wildfire. When Sam Barton heard it, he roared like a mad bull, and sent for Stud Walters and Tico Jones.

They came up to the house where Barton was waiting on them. "Take the kid with yuh an' drift intuh town. Find Cooper an' box him in. Pick a fight with him any way yuh kin an' cut him down. I want him Dead! You understand, DEAD, an' thet Sheriff too. I got plans an' they aire in my way!"

"What kind of plans Sam," Stud asked?"

"I plan tuh take over this whole Damn range," Barton told him with a snap of his wolfish teeth!

After locating the Kid, the trio mounted up and rode into town, coming in from separate ways. Now they would start earning their gun wages. Stud took one side of the street and Tico took the other, strolling along like they didn't have a care in the world. But their hot eyes probed every window, doorway and alley, searching from under their pulled down hat brims. This was the way they worked, like two hungry Coyotes looking for a meal.

Kid Cody rode straight to the Crystal Palace. Tying his horse at the hitch-rail outside, swaggered inside like he owned the place. The interior was cool and dark after being out in the hot sun. Stepping up to the bar, he ordered a whiskey with a beer chaser, his snake like eyes roaming around the barn sized room. Suddenly he stiffened, and his heart pounded in his skinny chest. Across the room, at a corner table, talking to the beautiful red haired woman who owned the place, sat the man he was sent to find. His job was to spot him if he was here, then signal Stud and Tico, but he wanted that job all for himself. To be known as the man who killed Harlan Cooper, the famed 'Widow Maker'! That was what buzzed through his distorted mind. To be famous! People would walk wide of him after that. Men would tip their hats, and the women would make eyes at him from behind their men's backs. His name would be known throughout the west! He would be somebody! He could see himself now, giving his version of the shooting to the newspaper, being toasted in saloons, picking any gunfighter job he wanted. Kid Cody, the man who killed the 'Widow Maker'. He could write his own ticket! Completely forgetting why he was here and all about Sam Barton, Stud and Tico, he stepped into the middle of the room. He didn't need anyone to back him, he was Kid Cody, fast gun. He licked his dry lips. Bending forward he opened his mouth.

"Cooper, I am callin' yuh out!" he yelled in his reedy voice.

Harlan looked up. Kid Cody was facing him, standing with his feet spread apart, a crazy expression in his narrow, hazel colored eyes, hands poised over his guns like two hawk claws. Damn. He was being braced by the crazy little gunman. Shannon got up and moved to the foot of the stairs, her eyes wide.

"That's right lady, move away from him. I would not like tuh see thet pretty dress git splattered with blood," he almost shouted.

Harlan rose as she backed up the stairs a few steps. She threw a frightened glance at him, but he stood there a half smile on his face.

The bartender and the five men there in the room, moved out of the line of fire.

The Kid laughed then, a wild crazy sound that sounded unearthly in the almost silent room. Looking Harlan up and down he snorted;

"Yuh don't look all that tough tuh me old man. The rest uv the men aire afraid tuh call yuh out Cooper, but not me, cause I am faster than yuh ever wuz, an' I am goin' tuh kill yuh Cooper. Me, Kid Cody, I will be known as the man who killed the 'Widow Maker," his voice sounding shrill and reedy in the huge room, as he laughed again.

"How are you goin' to kill me Kid, worry me to death," Harlan's cold, voice calm and carrying across the space between them.

The room got so quiet you could have heard a pin drop. There was a sound of heavy breathing, outside a horse stamped his hooves, rattling his bridle. The Kid stood there poised, enjoying the show he was putting on. People would talk about it for weeks to come, how he shot down the 'Widow Maker'. Hell, he would be as famous as Billy The Kid. His skinny five foot nine inch frame looked too frail to hold up the tied down .45 Colts slung low on his hips, but he was known to be fast as a striking rattler with them.

"Go tuh Hell Cooper," he laughed, snorting through his nose.

"You first Kid," Harlan said in his quiet voice.

The men who saw it, said the Kid's guns were just coming out of their holsters when a shot rang out. The Kid flew backwards, his spurs digging in the floor as his body arched, then lay still. Harlan stood reloading his gun as onlookers gathered around his limp body. Everyone swore they only heard one shot, but when the Doctor opened his shirt, the Kid had two holes through his heart less than an inch apart.

A crowd had gathered in the room and there was a hubbub of voices. Stud and Tico heard the gunfire, and came running. They eased up to the saloon doors peering over the doors. Inside they saw the Kid stretched out on the floor dead. The man they were hunting, Cooper, stood with the woman who owned the place, now his wife, with his arm around her. They slipped away through the crowd and rode back to the Box B.

Soon the news of the shooting was all over town, and folks

stared at Harlan in awe. He had just killed one of the top gunslingers around and did it with ease. The men who witnessed it swore they never saw Harlan's arm move his draw was so fast. He was standing there with that smile on his face, then a gun was in his hand spitting leaden death.

Later, up in their rooms, Harlan took Shannon in his arms feeling her tremble as she hugged him tightly.

"I was scared Harlan, everybody knew he was crazy and lighting with a gun."

"Don't worry about me honey, I have went up against better men than him."

"What will happen now? Will they try to kill you again?"

"Probably. But I look for Barton to declare war in earnest now. The sooner it starts, the sooner it will be over."

"Hold me tight Harlan," she whispered as a shudder ran through her body.

When Lee told his wife about Harlan Cooper being his new Deputy, she was shocked at the news.

"Why did you pick him of all people", she asked?

"Because he is the man for the job," Lee told her. "Most folks just think of him as the 'Widow Maker', but he is a good man in a lot of ways. He knows how to handle the kind of men I am up against."

" I hope you have not made a mistake," she had replied.

Now she knew why Cooper was here. Or did she?

CHAPTER 8

Harlan sat in the Sheriff's office with Lee and Ed, a while after the shooting talking about it.

"It was a put up job Lee. I caught a glimpse of Walters an' Jones after the crowd gathered. He was send to locate me, then set me up in a cross fire for them, but the Kid thought he could take me by his self. By now they are all back at Bartons makin' new plans."

"Why you an' not me," Lee asked?"

"Because I am the biggest threat to them an' their plans right now. But, I think that if they had killed me, you would have been next. With us out of the way, Barton would ride rough shod over everyone around, try to sew up the town. It is all coming to a head."

"I cannot go and arrest him just on suspicion, even though I would like to."

"He will make a move soon, an' we will have him. After what happened today, he knows we are watching him, an' he will move against us first."

"I suppose you are right Harlan, but I hate this sitting and watching."

"Don't worry Lee, things are about to bust wide open."

That evening Harlan sat with Shannon at supper in the upstairs kitchen of the Crystal Palace. Jilly had fixed them steaks smothered in mushrooms and onions, mashed potatoes, green beans with a big apple pie for desert. Harlan ate with a hearty appetite, but Shannon only picked at her food, and Jilly scolded her.

"Miss Shannon, you got to eat now, keep up your strength. You don't want to lose that fine figure of yours do you? Mister Harlan wouldn't like that at all. No mam he wouldn't."

Shannon smiled at her. Jilly had been with her so long, she felt like her mother.

"No Jilly, I sure don't want to lose my figure. But I am just not hungry tonight."

"Well, Mr Harlan shore ain't lost his appitite. That's his second piece of pie."

Harlan reached over and took her hand and she looked up at him with big soul-full eyes.

"I am tired of this waiting for something to happen," she said.

"That is part of the game Shannon, waiting for the other man to make his move."

"But it was never like this before Harlan, but then I never had this much to lose before either."

"Come on, let's go down stairs, it is almost time for your show."

"All right," she sighed, "but stay close to me."

"I will, I promise to stay by your side my love."

She thanked him with a look from her eyes. That night she sang her heart out, smiling at Harlan as he sat at his regular table. As soon as she was through, she came over to his table and whispered in his ear. He stood and they went upstairs to their rooms where Shannon fell in his arms covering his face with kisses. Harlan carried her into the bedroom, where they undressed in the semi-darkness. They lay in bed, Shannon curled up in his arms, her head on his chest never wanting to let him go!

The next day Owen Straight came into the Sheriff's office stomping mad, his face red and hot with rage. His foreman followed him in, a sling around his left arm.

Before anyone could say a word he bellowed out, "they hit us again last night by Gawd!"

"Who hit you," Lee asked although he knew the answer to his question.

"Barton an' his crew, thet's who! Burned one uv my barns, shot up the bunk house, an' ranch house, an' wounded two uv my men, one serious!"

"You know it was Barton for sure?"

"Hell yes. I seen him plain as day, him an' them gunmen uv his!"

"Don't you have two gunmen on your payroll Straight?"

"Yeah, I hired a couple, an' hadn't been fer them we woulda been caught flat footed. Fight fire with fire I say! What yuh figgerin' on doin' about it Sheriff?"

"Swear out a complaint, an' I will go out and serve it on him. Talk to him about last night."

"Talk Hell, I want him arrested an' put in jail!"

"I will do what I can do Straight."

"The rest uv my crew aire comin' intuh town bringin' the wounded in a wagon. We aire gonna wait around hyar fer yuh tuh come back Sheriff."

Harlan sat and listened to Barton as he told of the raid, his hands by his sides knotted into hard fists, his barrel chest rising and falling as he poured out his passionate story, finally running down. Signing the piece of paper Lee handed him, he stormed out of the office with his foreman in tow. Lee folded the paper, put it in his pocket, and glanced over at Harlan.

"I think we have a case now again Barton, if it sticks."

"It will stick all right."

Lee got up and put on his hat, "Well, let's ride."

Out at Barton's ranch a rider came galloping in trailing dust behind him, sliding his horse to a stop where Barton and the rest of the crew stood in front of the long low bunk house. The sweaty rider grinned at Barton.

"Just like you figgured Boss, Straight an' his foreman hev gone tuh town, an' the rest aire follerin' in with a wagon carryin' the shot up un's."

Barton was a man on fire. He wanted Straight's ranch and water, but to get it he must do away with Straight. With him and that Cooper gunslinger gone, the Sheriff and his other Deputy would be easy, like taking candy from a baby. The law was too far away to be of any help to the town's people and they knew it. The only law within over a hundred miles was the Sheriff and the two Deputy's. The town could be buffaloed. He would put in one of his men as Sheriff and two more as Deputy's, then the town would fold. He would make sure no word was sent out. If the law ever did come in sniffing around, the town's folk would be too scared to talk by then.

He looked his crew over. Twenty handpicked hard riders, counting the two hired guns, Stud and Tico. They missed their chance at Cooper before on account of that damm fool Kid, but he was as good as dead. To Hell with him and his fast guns. Not many people knew it, but he was damn good with a gun himself. This wouldn't be the first time he had killed a man over a ranch. The trouble was then that the law had been too close and he had to ride out ahead of a posse. But here, the law was a long ways off. His thin lips curled back in a wolfish smile, his tobacco stained teeth showing. But it wasn't really a smile, just a slight curling of the lips. He looked across the shimmering range, soon it would all be his!

"Mount Up," he shouted, "we aire headin' fer town!"

Lee, Harlan and Ed were on their way to Bartons ranch, when they saw the cloud of yellow dust. Pulling their horses off into a clump of rocks, Lee pulled out his glass and took a long look, as did Harlan, who pulled his binoculars from his saddle bags studying the bunched riders.

"I make it to be twenty or better. Hard to get a good count through the dust. What do you make it Lee?"

"About the same, maybe twenty, maybe more."

"All armed to the teeth. I can see the sunlight reflectin' off their guns!"

Putting his spy glass away, Lee said, "heading straight for town! They are ready to start a war!"

Harlan agreed. "Straight an' what's left of his crew are in town, an' Barton knows it. Seems like Barton is bringin' the fight to us. Figgers to wipe us all out in one swipe I recon. Let's get an' make ready for him!"

They turned the horses, heading back to town, riding well ahead of Barton and his crew. Arriving at Twin Rivers, they tied up their horses in front of the Sheriff's office and Lee told Ed to warn the town's people about the oncoming fight.

"Tell them to lock the doors and stay inside, unless they want to get a gun and back us!"

"Think any uv 'em will Sheriff?"

Lee gave a harsh laugh. "I doubt it Ed, I seriously doubt it."

Straight and his foreman came rushing up. "What's happenin' Sheriff?"

Barton and his crew are on their way to town loaded for bear Owen!"

Straight stroked his chin. "I hev six men hyar includin' Slade an' Hardin. They aire all over at the Crystal Palace. I'll go over thar an' tell 'em tuh git ready!"

"Hold it Straight, No shooting until I give the word," Lee ordered, "understand!"

Owen Straight gave him a hard look from his dark piercing eyes, but agreed. He turned on his heel and made for the saloon, followed closely by his foreman.

"I need to get over there myself," Harlan said, "an' talk to Shannon, plus pick up my extra guns."

Lee watched him cross the street, then headed for his home at a fast walk. The fight was on its way sure as God made little green apples and he wanted to kiss his wife, hug his son, to assure them everything would be all right, even though he wasn't sure of anything at all.

Harlan stood in the almost empty barroom facing Straight and his men. Shannon stood on the stairs listening, her hand gripping the rail, watching him, so tall and sure of himself, so unafraid of what was coming. Gunfights were just part of his world, the world he had lived in for years alone. But now he had her and the life they planned. She could feel her heart beating sluggish in her breast, the fear for him like a raw wound inside her. But she must not show her fear. She must be strong for him, lend him her strength. Harlan was speaking to the men.

"When Barton gets here, Lee will try to talk reason to him. I don't think it will do any good, but he has to try anyway. After that, if shootin' starts, it is every man for hisself. After that, if any of you men have a axe to grind with me, I will be available!"

Jim Slade looked at Harlan with a half grin, "I want yuh tuh know thet me an' Brown hev no designs on yuh atall. We wuz hired tuh fight Barton, not you."

Brown dipped his head, "thet's right Harlan."

"Thanks Jim, that takes a load off my mind," Harlan laughed.

Slade chuckled, "I will jist bet it did."

"When this is over Jim, maybe I can buy you an' Brown a drink."

"We look forward tuh it Harlan."

The men filed out then, taking up positions along the street. Jim Slade stopped by Harlan.

"Whut do yuh want me an' Brown tuh do?"

Harlan grinned and laid his hand on Slade's shoulder. "I think you know what to do Jim, you an' Brown both. You are a good man Jim, you will do to ride the river with, an' so will Brown." Harlan had an easy going way about him with these kind of men. Men a lot like himself.

Slade inclined his head, a smile creasing his weathered face, "luck Harlan."

Shannon ran to Harlan ran to hug him tightly. "Be careful my darling," she whispered, "don't let anything happen to you out there."

"I will be careful my love, but sometimes cold nerve carries a man like me through better than caution. After I am gone, lock up tight, go upstairs to our rooms an' wait for me there."

"All right darling, I will. Kiss me before you go."

Harlan pulled her close to kiss her red trembling lips, and she clung to him, her lips trying to hold him as he pulled away, yet knowing she couldn't. This was something he must do, face up to danger as he had always done, calm and sure. Depending on no one or nothing but his skill with a gun and cold nerve. Releasing her, he checked his guns to make sure they were all fully loaded, then stepped out onto the board walk pulling the doors shut behind him. Seeing Lee standing in the middle of the street, walked over to join him, noticing that he carried a ten gauge Express shotgun in the crook of his arm. Harlan pointed to the big gun, "loaded for bear huh?"

"Barton reminds me more of a wolf that a bear, but probably hard to kill as a bear."

Harlan also noticed he was wearing two Colts, and on both belts the loops were full of shells for them. Ed was standing in the office door with a Henry rifle and Harlan knew there was another one by his side. There were men at the livery stable, and some behind boxes stacked on the store porch. Not a member of the town of Twin Rivers was in sight. They were all behind locked doors afraid to make a stand behind their sheriff, for they knew that if the Sheriff and his men failed to stop Barton and his crew, they would turn on the town. Harlan glanced around noting everything. Well, they were as prepared, as ready as they would ever be. A sound of horses came to him and he saw them then coming down the street from the west, spread out like calvary soldiers. It looked like a few of the town hanger-ons had joined Barton. People liked to back a winner. They looked to be a salty bunch, twenty four or five men, heavily armed just spoiling for a fight. Fifty feet from Lee and himself, they drew rein, sitting their saddles, staring, mean looks on their faces.

From an upstairs window, Shannon watched Barton and his crew as they rode in to stop in front of Harlan and the Sheriff. Her eyes were glued on Harlan's tall figure as he stood there watching Barton. On her lips was a prayer for him and their life ahead, if there was one later.

CHAPTER 9

Just outside of town, Barton had halted his riders to give them final instructions in his hoarse voice.

"When we git in thar, spread out. The ones we want tuh git first aire Straight, the Sheriff, an' Cooper, er the 'Widow Maker' as some call him!"

Stud Walters spoke up; "Me an' Tico will take him, we hev a score tuh settle. Cooper will be oure meat!"

Barton helt up a big paw. "All right, take 'im if yuh kin, but the rest uv us will be shootin' too! Make shore uv them three an' any others will jist be a bonus! Now lets ride!"

Lee and Barton faced each other in the dusty, hot street. A sudden light wind stirred a small bit of the dust settling it against the side walk. An old yellow hound that had been laying there in the slight shade, got up with his tail between his legs and slunk off into an alley. Straight and his men were scattered along the side walk watching to see what Barton would do. He sat in his saddle, rawboned, tough, roughhewn, both of his big hairy hands on his saddle horn. He looked everybody over, his sharp, hot glance moving from one to the other as he sized them up.

"Wal, looks like everybody's hyar. Lookee thar boys, all in one pile," he told them as he pointed a crooked finger.

Some of the men behind snickered at the remark.

Lee's voice rang out in the crowded street, "what do you want Barton?"

Barton's lips peeled back like an animals with that wolfish imatation of a smile. "I want you Sheriff, an' you Cooper, an' you Straight!" His voice boomed in the quiet street, as his finger pointed again.

"When I am through with you, I will own this town! Have my own Sheriff an' laws!"

"You are crazy Barton," Lee's flat reply rang out!

Barton threw back his head to roared with laughter. "I hev enough men tuh ride this town in the dirt! Listen all yuh men thet ride fer Straight, eny uv yuh thet want tuh git out of this fight, jist go to the end of town at Madame Caroline's 'hore house an' wait fer me! I will hire yuh tuh ride fer me after the fight! When I take over Straight's ranch, I will need more riders!"

A long minute ticked away, but not a man moved nor answered his offer,

"Then take the same medicine thet I am goin' tuh give yore boss an' the Sheriff thar," he roared!

Lee brought his shotgun up. "You are under arrest Barton, you an' all your men!"

While Barton had been talking, Stud and Tico moved their horses closer to where Harlan stood, his hand hanging loosely at his sides. He watched them, almost smiling.

"Yuh ain't arrestin' me Sheriff, not today er ever, Barton shouted as he dived off his horse!

The big ten gauge shotgun in Lee's hands roared as he dived, the double ought buckshot missing him but hitting two riders behind him, knocking them off their horses and into the hard street. Dropping the shotgun, he pulled both Colt .45's shooting left and right. Pandemonium broke out in the street then as men jumped or fell from bucking horses, guns blasted, gunsmoke filled the street and bullets sang their death songs as they bit into flesh. Harlan's Colts were singing a song of their own as he cut loose on Stud and Tico. Three bullets from Harlan's Colts plowed into Tico's chest, he swayed in his saddle, then fell lifeless on the ground limp and bloody. Stud jumped his horse at Harlan almost causing him to miss his shot. His bullet hit the saddle horn glancing up and ripping across Stud's chest and through his shoulder. He half fell, half jumped from his mount landing beside a water trough, his gun firing. Harlan felt the slug strike him in the side gouging out a grove as he shoot into Stud again, knocking him down. Two men ran their horses at him, and he emptied his Colts into them driving them backwards. One fell off and the other rode away hanging over his horse's neck. Cool and calm in the face of death, he dropped the empty Colts into their holsters and drew two more. He turned to see Lee reloading just as Barton staggered from behind a porch post, his guns trained on Lee. Harlan sprang forward just as Barton fired, the bullet striking him in the chest. He pumped four slugs into Barton knocking him off his feet to lie bloody and still on the side walk. Lee was down. Harlan didn't know how bad he was hit, if he was hurt bad or not. A bullet hit him in the back, turning him to see Stud standing by the water trough, blood streaming from his wounds steadying his gun for another shot. Harlan was shooting with both hands, his bullets striking Stud, driving him back. Harlan felt another slug strike him as Stud died on his feet. As he staggered backwards, another bullet struck him, and he emptied his guns into the man.

Shannon was mesmerized as she watched the fight below her. Harlan and the Sheriff seemed to be in the thick of it! Tears ran down her cheeks as she stood by the window, her hands clenched at her breast. Jilly stood behind her, hands on Shannon's shoulders as she watched the bloody scene in the street.

"Do you see Mr Harlan child?"

"No! Wait, there he is! He is staggering! Oh Jilly, he has been shot! He is falling down! He is hurt bad! I must go to him!"

She tore loose from Jilly's grip and picking up her dress bottom, ran out of the room and down the stairs toward the front door.

The sound of gun fire was slacking off as Harlan sat down heavily, fumbling as he tried to reload his guns. He saw Barton lying on his back, half of his face shot away. Harlan's hands felt clumsy. He saw a Box B rider standing in the street, a pistol in his right hand, his left clutched against his chest where a stream of blood gushed. He blinked at Harlan, swaying like a tree in the wind. His gun was too heavy for him to hold any longer and he dropped it as he went to his knees, falling over, raising a cloud of dust around him. Harlan finally got one of his colts loaded as he tried to get to his feet, then sat back staring at the blood on his chest and arms. He saw Stud lying there dead. Harlan's last bullet had sliced through his throat, the big .44 slug almost decapitating him. Suddenly he felt weak and dizzy. Attempted to reload his gun but lacked the strength. It felt awful heavy, something was wrong with his hands and eyes! The ground spun around him. He heard voices. Someone calling his name. Who? Other voices came to him but he couldn't understand what they were saying.

The street got dark, as the ground rushed up to meet him. He rolled over and stared at the sky. Must be getting ready to rain the sky was so dark. Someone called his name again. A face close to his. A beautiful face with green eyes. A smell of perfume. Who? Did Angels wear perfume? Someone kissed him and called his name over and over. The face faded as a red mist settled over him. Peaceful. Still. Was this how it felt to die? He felt weightless, almost floating. So peaceful and calm. All sounds and faces drifted away from him as the world closed up around him, and he slowly faded away.

A soft breeze moved the curtains at the window, as in the bed there, a man with bandages on his chest and arm lay sleeping. From the way he moaned and groaned it was not a peaceful sleep. A woman tiptoed into the room to check him. His face was still flushed but not as hot to the touch. Good. The fever was receding. She removed the warm cloth from his fore head, rung it out in cool water replacing it there. His breathing was shallow but steady. The hands laying on top of the bed covering had blue veins showing through the whiteness of them. Other than occasional groans, he had not uttered a word all the time he lay there. The woman bent over and kissed his fever blistered lips softly, then stood at the end of the bed wiping tears from her eyes as she turned to leave. The door closed gently behind her. Lee looked at her as she came out of the bedroom, his left arm in a sling.

"Any change?"

Shannon sadly shook her head. "No, not that much, although I believe the fever is leaving him. But he seems the same as before."

"He saved my life," Lee said. "If he hadn't stepped in between me an' Barton's gun, he would have killed me. I saw it in his eyes as I was trying to reload. Barton had me cold. Harlan jumped between us killing Barton takin' the slug meant for me. I owe him my life!"

Lee's wife Sara spoke up. "He is a strong man, a good man, he will live, I know it!"

Shannon dropped into a chair beside her. "My life and my future is lying in there fighting for his life. I can't lose him, not after all the years of waiting, hoping and praying. No, he can't die, he just can't!"

Sara patted her hand. "Dr Clark was a surgeon during the war and he says he is strong, that he has a fighting chance. He is a fighter as we all know."

"Yes, he is a fighter," Shannon said softly.

There was a knock on the door and Sara opened it to admit Sandy Wells, Shannon's good friend.

"How is he today," she asked?, coming over to hug Shannon.

"About the same. He just seems to be wasting away Sandy, day by day."

"The preacher at the church has been saying prayers for him. Everybody in town is pulling for him Shannon and the girls at the Palace want to know if there is anything they can do to help."

"No. But thank them for me."

"Don't worry about anything except getting him well. Between me and Henry, we have everything under control for you. We are running it just like you would if you were there."

She hugged Shannon again and left. Shannon had not been at the Crystal Palace since Harlan was shot. She had Sandy bring her some clothes sleeping on a cot by Harlan's bed every night watching over him.

Three days later Dr Clark visited Harlan as he had every day since he had been here. Shannon was sitting by his bedside, trying to read, watching him closely. He was breathing easier now and the Doctor said he was improving. His face didn't look so pale as before. As she sat there willing him to come back to her and calling his name softly, his eyelids fluttered. Shannon gasped. They fluttered again, then slowly opened. He stared up into her startled face.

"Shannon," he whispered weakly.

She touched his face with trembling hands. "Harlan! You are awake at last," she said with tears streaming down her face. "After all this time of waiting and praying, my God darling, you are awake!"

A small smile touched his face. "Where am I?"

"At Lee's house. He had them bring you here so he could be with you day and night in case you needed him. At first the Doctor thought you were dead, but you still had a heartbeat. He, I, Lee and

Sara worked with you all through that first long night. Dr Clark took six bullets out of you darling. We sat up with you those first few nights when you were fighting for your life. Those long, dark, terrible nights when we thought every breath would be your last. But you lived my darling, you lived," she told him with tears running down her thin cheeks.

"Don't cry my love, I am gettin' well now."

She laid her damp cheek against his, and lay like that for several minutes letting her sorrow drain away.

"How is Lee," he asked? turning his head slightly on the thick pillow.

"He is good. A bullet went through his shoulder and knocked him down. He said you saved his life by stepping in front of him and taking the bullets from Barton's gun meant for him."

"Just keepin' my promise made long ago."

"I know dear, and so does his wife now."

"Lee's wife an' son. I have never met them."

"Harlan honey, do you think you should talk so much?"

"I feel better, just weak, an' I am hungry."

"I will get you some broth dear."

"Broth, I want a steak an' about a dozen eggs."

She smiled at that and kissed his cheek.

"You have not eaten anything since the fight darling except a few spoons of broth I managed to feed you. No wonder you are starved."

"How long has that been?"

"Over two weeks."

He seemed surprised, "that long?"

"Seventeen long days my darling you have lain here fighting fever and infection, trying to stay alive."

He lay silent for a few minutes.

"Call Lee, his wife an' son in. It is time I met them."

At Shannon's call Lee and his wife came into the room to stand by his bedside. Wyatt stood in the doorway staring, his eyes wide.

"Help me sit up," Harlan told them in a soft voice.

They carefully got him into a sitting position with several pillows behind him.

He looked around. "I will be all right now, so you all can quit worrying."

Lee took his hand. "I owe you my life brother."

Harlan looked up at him. "You told them?"

"I told everybody. Every person knows that you are my older brother. I would not have it any other way. When I saw you laying there with Barton's bullets in you, the bullets meant for me, and thought you were dead, I felt ashamed we had to go by different names. I told them who you were. Surprised the Hell out of them I can tell you that. The Mayor wanted to know why our names were not the same. I told them Cooper was your middle name, our Mother's name. That you dropped your last name on account of me, to keep people with a grudge against you away from me. That your right name is Harlan Coulter, my brother. That set them to talking."

"Something else, then I will go an' let you rest Harlan. About a week after the shootout, a Texas Ranger rode in here. He was looking for a man fitting Barton's description up this way. Seems like Barton was wanted for murder down in the Panhandle. Killed a rancher there and took over his ranch. Then he killed a Sheriff who come out to investigate. Left there two jumps ahead of the Rangers, and they been looking for him ever since. He was glad to hear he was dead, and wanted to meet the man who killed him. But I told him that the man who killed him, Harlan Cooper, was also killed in the shootout. We showed him Barton's grave, also the one with your name on it."

Harlan stared at his brother, "my grave?"

"Yeah. We buried you and your reputation on the evening of the fight. All the town's people and Straight took a solemn oath they would never tell. By the way, Straight has been around here to see you a couple of times. Wants to make up for the way he acted before."

"So, I am dead an' buried," he mused, a small grin on his face.

"Yep. From now on you will be just plain James Coulter."

"James. That was Pa's name," Harlan replied, nodding his head

"I think Pa would like you to use it, now that you are starting over. That Ranger knew you Harlan, and said you never was as black as people painted you."

Shannon bent and kissed his forehead. "Now we can do all those things we planned, James Coulter."

He smiled at her glowing face.

"One last thing to tell you then I will let you be brother", Lee said. "Barton's ranch will be coming up for sale later on if you two are interested."

Shannon asked Harlan what he thought of the idea living here at Twin Rivers.

"Well if Harlan Cooper is dead, I see no reason James Coulter couldn't be a rancher here." he looked at Lee. "What do you think Sheriff?"

"Yes, I think he could become a respectable rancher with a little help," Lee replied with a laugh.

Sara came over to Harlan, bending over, giving him a sisterly kiss. "Thank you for saving my husband's life Harlan, you have fulfilled your promise and now you deserve some happiness of your own. The both of you," she told them as she came around to hug Shannon

Harlan looked slightly uncomfortable at her words and everyone left then but Shannon. His beautiful wife. She sat beside him ruffling his hair.

"James. I guess I had better get used to calling you that now, don't you think?"

"It is a good solid name," he replied.

"Yes, solid, like you are my darling. What do you think about buying Barton's ranch James?"

"Well, now that Harlan Cooper is dead, James Coulter could be a rancher, or a business man, or a gambler, or.."

Shannon put her hand over his mouth. "Rancher," she whispered.

He squeezed her hand. "You wouldn't mind living here?"

"No, not at all. We would be close to your brother and his wife."

"It would be a good place to raise some cattle, horses, and kids."

He looked into her smoky green eyes as she leaned down to kiss him. His past was gone, buried forever, but the future looked bright ahead......

THE END.

A MAN'S WORK.

      Will Thurman looked down at the cast on his left leg in disgust. His broken ribs were beginning to heal, but this bed had been his prison for the better part of a month now and he was tired of it. Why did it have to happen now? Now that he had the best bounty of timber to cut in the whole county. He knew why, he had been in too much of a hurry and turned his T-D Nine International Crawler over on a rocky hill. It threw him out of the seat and rolled over him. The only thing that saved his life was the fact that he landed in a low spot in the rocks and only got his left leg broken in three places and four broken ribs. He had just started logging on the tract when the accident happened. His son Billy had found him lying there. With the help of Ted Long, his long-time friend/ timber cutter, they got him out, loaded into his pickup and to the Gray County Hospital at Martinville. Dr Smith said he would be laid up for four months, that he may never walk right again. Will cussed as he lay there in the hospital bed in his living room watching television. Damm the luck anyway! He had to get back in the woods! The tract must be finished by December thirty first, and it was the middle of May now. He had borrowed money for two new saws and a rubber tired loader, a good used 3444 International loader with forks and bucket to load the logs with. His old one being worn completely out, along with having his two ton G-M-C log truck overhauled and new brakes put on it. How would he pay back that money at the bank? The note would be due the first of January. He cussed some more.

      His wife of eighteen years, Madge, came in to check on him.

      "Are you hurting Will? I thought I heard you calling me."

"No, just mad at myself for gettin' in a rush. All that timber to cut and here I lay on my ass all busted up!"

"It could have been a lot worse Will. You know that."

"Yes Madge, I know that it could have, but dammit if we don't get that timber out before the first of the year, we stand to lose everything we have worked for all these years!

"Billy and Ted are working every day on it."

"I know, but I need to be with them. Tom is a good man, but Billy is only a boy yet, not able to take all that responsibility on his shoulders."

Billy had been helping log on weekends while he went to school, but now that his father was laid up, he had taken time off from his studies to help Ted get the tract cut out. The Principal of Martinville high school agreed to let him make up his schoolwork at his own pace and attend summer school to finish out his grades. It was a load for a sixteen year old boy to take on his shoulders, but he had no choice. He must help his parents, there was no one else.

Madge smiled at him. "He has been in the woods with you since he could walk Will, always in your hip pocket."

He grinned. "Yeah. That boy is a worker all right. If I could hire another man to help them, but every able bodied man around here is up to his ears in work."

"Things will work out hon, I know they will."

"I hope you are right Madge, I sure hope so."

That night as Billy came in the house for supper, he looked worn out, with a deep frown on his face.

"What's wrong son, "Will asked?

"Bud Small came out and looked over the Crawler this afternoon and said it would be better to buy a new one than fix it."

"Is it that bad?"

"Well Dad, one track is torn loose plus the adjustment is broken, the manifold is broken off, and when it hit on its side, a sharp rock busted the block and tearing the injection pump and lines off. Other than that it is in good shape."

As bad as the news was, Will had to grin at that.

"So, he says it is not worth fixing. I suppose we could use the loader to drag out in a pinch, but it don't have a winch on it. How much did Bud say it would cost to fix it?"

"The way he talked several thousand dollars."

Will frowned at that, and cussed some more.

"Dad, I had an idea on the way home."

"What's that son?"

"My shop class at school is always looking for a project to work on, how about letting them have a crack at the Crawler?"

"Hum, not a bad idea. Art Hays has some parts left off his old Crawler, and there are some scattered around here. Yeah. Talk to them, find out if they are interested in doin' it and go from there."

"I'll call some of them tonight."

After supper, Billy called some of his classmates to explaine the situation to them. All of them were working part time, but said they would help in evenings and weekends, so Billy told them to meet him in the shop at his house tomorrow evening. Next day with chains and the help of the loader, Billy and Tom got the busted up T-D Nine on a trailer moving it down to the shop, putting it under the outside roof. That afternoon seven boys showed up to work staying until ten o'clock. There were all kinds of tools in the shop along with a cutting torch and a welder. They were all Billy's age of sixteen, shop trained, knowing their way around a motor and tools. Every evening Will lay in his bed watching them going at it from his window. Ted was marking trees, getting them ready to cut. If worse came to worse they could try to drag out some of the bigger logs with the loader. Already now Billy and Ted were dragging small logs out with the loader and chains. It was slow aggravating work doing that, but they had no choice. When they got a load on the truck Ted would take them to the mill while Billy drug out some more. Every morning Billy and Ted were in the woods at daylight, their big Stihl saws roaring. At dinner time they would stop long enough to gulp down a sandwich, a drink, then back to work. Billy's parents worried about him, but he just grinned and went on. On the weekends he helped the other boys repair the Crawler. They finished it up on a Sunday evening three weeks later with spare parts from here and there. Filling it up with Diesel, motor oil and antifreeze, Billy fired it up. It missed. One of the injectors wasn't working properly

The boys got busy and took it out, cleaned it, readjusted it, put it back in and when it started up again, ran like a top. Now it was fixed, but they were so far behind, work would have to go on seven days a week now. Will was worried and watched the boys working on the crawler wishing he could be out there. The doctor said he should be able to ride in a wheelchair in three to four more weeks without doing any harm to his leg, but he felt as though he had been in the cast for half his life. Billy and Ted were going full blast in the woods now, working from can see to can't see, but still the going was slow.

Billy came in after dark, ate his supper, showered and went to bed. His mother got up early every morning and fixed breakfast. Will ate with them talking to Billy about things he should know about cutting in the woods and things to watch for. They had cut most of the logs now that were to go to Taylor's sawmill, and were ready to start on the veneer logs. That was where the money was. On the back of the tract was a huge stand of Walnut trees, most of them bigger than two men could reach around. Will was depending on them and the Red Oaks to bring in a tidy sum. Billy and Ted were cutting the Oaks now with a log buyer waiting to get them cut and yarded so he could stick them. Will had made a deal with the buyer to pick up the Red Oaks and Walnuts at the tract. He had already made a good sized log yard near the front of the tract to yard them up in. Now here he was laid up, and he cussed some more.

Will Thurman had sawdust in his veins. His father and grandfather had been loggers and it was a life he loved. As soon as he could get around on crutches he meant to go out there to at least watch them drag the logs out. A new red Ford pickup came creeping up into the front of the house and stopped at the yard gate. The driver's door opened and a well dressed man got out. He looked around, came through the yard gate and toward the house. Clark Gray, the banker at Martinville Bank, Savings and Loan. He walked upon the porch knock on the kitchen door. Madge opened it and bade him good morning.

"Morning Madge, how are you?"

"Oh, fine I recon Clark. Yourself?"

"O K as far as I know."

"Come in Clark, Will is in the living room."

He walked into the sunny room to find Will sitting up in bed. "How you feeling Will?'

"How do I look?"

Clark studied him for a moment. "Looks like you are tired of lying there Will."

"I am. Dammed tired of it," Will laughed.

Clark laughed along with him. "How long has it been now?"

"Six weeks and four days."

Clark sat down in a chair by the hospital bed, looking at Will. "What is Doc saying about your leg?"

"I should be up and around on crutches in a couple more weeks, but he says I may never walk right again."

"It's hard to keep a good man down Will. I know you. Won't be long until you are back in the woods dropping trees again."

"I wish I was there now Clark. Billy and Ted are working seven days a week to get the logs out before the deadline. It is working them into the ground, just them two"

"There is nobody around you could hire to help?"

"No, everybody is working. I have already tried to hire somebody."

"The last day of December is the deadline, right?"

"Yeah the tract has to be cut by then or I forfeit everything that is on the ground, cut or uncut. The log buyers want the logs piled as we cut so they can stick them and haul them out. If we are not done by the deadline, I lose everything."

Clark shook his head. He knew Will had put up his machinery and house for the collateral on the loan. He could stand to lose everything he owned, for he also had to put up a twenty five thousand dollar cash bond in case he failed at the job. Will was his friend and Clark was worried. The owners of the timber insisted on a cash bond to make sure the job was done on time. Will was a good man and a top logger, seeing no problem with the bond at the time. But now, laid up like he was, Clark knew he was worried about it.

"Will," he said, "you know I will do everything I can to help you. You also have a lot of good friends to help you out if it comes to that, but between me and you, do you think you can make it on time?"

After a minute of deep thought, Will shook his head. "Honestly Clark, I don't know. Ted is one of the best timber cutters in the business and has been with me for years. Billy is young and willing, but time is against us now that I am down."

"What if bad weather sets in Will?"

"Then I guess we will be moving," he replied, a tight smile on his face, looking over at his wife who stood in the kitchen door, a troubled expression on her face

CHAPTER 2

The fourth of July came on a Saturday that year. Billy and Ted took off a couple of days to rest up, but Billy spent most of his time checking the equipment and saws over. Preventive Maintenance he called it. It was the first time they had taken off since they started on the Borden Tract as it was called. Monday morning bright and early they were in the woods dropping trees, dragging them out. Ted would fell the tree, cut it to full log length and Billy would drag them out to the log yard. There they would be cut into the proper length and ricked for the buyer. He came every day and hauled out the logs on a tractor and trailer with Billy loading them for him for Red Oaks will bust open in warm weather if left laying very long. The buyer hauled them to the big mill owned by Lawton Lumber and Veneer Company. There they were kept wet by water sprayed over them twenty four hours a day.

It kept Ted and Billy humping to get out a trailer load every day, but they always made it. There was a lot riding on them and they worked like giants at it. The crawler began to overheat one day bringing in a drag. Billy knew the radiator was leaking, maybe stopped up. As soon as the load of logs went out that evening, he got the toolbox and with Ted's help drained out the antifreeze taking the leaky radiator off. The bottom seam was cracked, also one of the veins had a hole in it. They loaded it on the 4x4 Ford three quarter ton pickup taking it into the shop. Laying it on some metal horses, Billy fired up the old steam-ginny, steaming off the dirt and oil off it.

"Gonna take a while to fix that leak," Ted said after looking it over.

"Yeah, I need to run down to the parts store and get some more solder. Why don't you go on home Ted, I can fix this tonight, it is a one man job anyway."

"Well, all right, if you think you can handle it Billy. I will go on to the house and sharpen up the saws tonight. See you in the morning."

Billy went into the house to tell his father what had happened, grabbed a sandwich and ran out the backdoor. Getting into the pickup, he headed for the parts store. He came back with solder and acid to clean the core vein and the brass bottom with. After cleaning it with that, he wiped it off and got out a bottle of red-hot sauce. It cleaned the brass until it shone bright as new. Taking up a torch he put a number two tip in it and fired it up. First he patched the hole in the core, the torch in his right hand, the solder in his left. Then he stood the radiator up clamping it to the metal horse and started on the bottom seam. It was a time consuming job, because the solder kept melting in front of where he was soldering. Finally getting a bit on the aggravated side, he brushed and cleaned the whole bottom, then ran the hot solder all the way around. At last he had it sealed. He put the tools away and carried the radiator out and put it in the bed of the pickup. He glanced at his watch to see that it was almost two thirty. No wonder he was tired, he had been up since five that morning. Wiping his hands on a shop towel, he shut the doors making his way tiredly his way to the house.

When his alarm went off at five that morning, Billy groaned, stretching his aching body. He got up to shower in water as cold as he could stand it. As he was drying off, heard his mother moving around in the kitchen. When he came out in his work clothes, she had breakfast ready. His father sat at the table sipping coffee and watching the morning news as he had ever since Billy could remember, except now he sat in a wheelchair. He looked up with a smile.

"Morning son."

"Morning Dad, Mom."

His mother turned from the stove where she was frying eggs and gave him a bright smile.

"You seem worn out this morning Billy. Did you get any sleep at all last night?"

"Couple hours," he yawned.

"I am going in to see Dr Smith this morning for a checkup. Maybe he will let me out for some fresh air," Will said.

"Don't push yourself Dad."

"Son, I am going crazy sittin' around here. Now I know what people mean by cabin fever."

Billy laughed. "I would be glad to trade places with you for a couple of days."

His mother sat breakfast on the table. Billy gobbled his up and grabbing the lunch box she handed him, was out the door and gone.

"That boy," Madge said as she watched him leave, "he is going to catch himself coming or going one of these days. Come on Will, let's get you ready for your appointment. Maybe you will come back on crutches."

Dr Justin Smith was a tall confident man of fourty three, with curly brown hair, brown eyes, and an easy smile. He had just given Will a checkup explaining to him how the leg was mending. He could use crutches now as long as he didn't overdo it. That point he stressed.

"Get out Will and move around some, but no lifting, driving or anything of that nature. Madge?"

"I'll see to it doctor that he doesn't overdo it."

The nurse brought in a set of crutches and Dr Smith fitted them to suit Will, having him walk around with them, trying them out. The exam over, Will hobbled out of the office and over to the Buick car of Madge's, sliding into the seat, a big smile on his face. Madge got in beside him, to start the motor, glancing over at him, a happy look on her face. He seemed to be his old self again.

"Take me out to the tract," he told Madge, "I want to see how they are doing."

She drove out of town on 327 and turned off about five miles out onto a dirt road. Following it about a mile and a half, she came to the big log yard, parking there under a shady oak. Will got out and sniffed the air like a hound on the trail. He swung his way over to the log pile where he sat down on a cut off block smiling from ear to ear. The sound of a crawler caught his ear. Turning he saw to see Billy coming out with a drag of logs. The smell of Diesel smoke came to him along with the scent of fresh cut logs. Billy saw him sitting there and waved, bringing the crawler to a stop near where he sat. He climbed out of the cab and came over where his father was.

"Hey dad, see you got your crutches."

"Yeah, feels good to get out of that damm wheelchair."

"What did the doctor say?"

"He said for him to take it easy for a while longer, but here he is like he can't wait to get back in that crawler again," his mother answered.

Will had a sheepish grin on his face.

"Don't worry Dad, me and Ted are coming along with the oaks."

"Yeah, but there are a lot of them back in there. You know that stand of Walnut is twice as big as the Red Oaks."

"You will soon be back in harness Will," Madge told him.

"I will be glad of it too. This is the biggest tract I have ever cut of Veneer logs. I am not worrying about Billy and Ted doing the work, but can they do it in time? What if they have another break down, or rainy weather sets in. I need to be here to help dammit!"

Billy glanced at his mother, she shook her head. Billy got back on the crawler and headed back into the woods after another drag. Madge got Will in the car under protest, taking him back home.

The next day Will got on his crutches and hobbled all around the yard, across the front lot, out to the shop and back. He was wet with sweat when he got back into the living room dropping into his comfortable chair, but he felt better. Madge had been watching him out the window as he moved about on the crutches. She noticed the determined look on his face as he walked. As he settled deeper into his comfortable chair, brought him a cold drink of water and he drank every drop.

"I am getting better Madge, I can feel it."

"Yes you are, but don't overdo it and hurt your leg."

He waved that off. "My leg is fine. Don't hardly hurt at all."

She left him and went back to her washing. It had been a big undertaking, borrowing all that money against their home, but she had always stood behind him in everything he did. Madge knew that if Will was able bodied, there would be no worry about paying off the loan, but deep inside her was a small knot of fear.

CHAPTER 3

Will walked every day until he began to tire out. A month later Dr Smith told him the cast could come off in two more weeks. It would be the middle of September. That would give him three and a half months to help get the timber out. He was looking forward to getting back in the woods to the smell of sawdust and diesel smoke. Finally the day came for him to go back to work. He was up at five o'clock that Monday morning, checking over the saws and cans of fuel. Madge called him in for breakfast and as he and Billy ate, she fixed their lunches. At six thirty they were in the woods gassing up the saws, fueling up the crawler and loader. At quarter of seven, Ted pulled in and got out of his Chevy pickup a big grin on his face.

"Good to see you back Will."

"It is good to be back Ted, I can tell you that. I have hung around the house so long, I got where I was liking the soap operas."

They had a laugh over that. Then Ted picked up his saw and fuel can, heading into the woods followed by Will. Billy checked the crawler over and fired it up. By the time he got back where the Red Oaks were, his father and Ted had a drag ready. It was like that all morning. After lunch, Will started cutting the logs into lengths and stacking them. At two in the afternoon, the Semi with its log trailer pulled in and Will loaded him out. As fast as Ted cut the trees down, Billy drug them out and Will cut and stacked them. As they made ready to leave that evening Will looked around proudly at the neatly stacked logs.

"Good days work. If the weather holds we should make the deadline easy enough. Think we should start earlier from now on Ted?"

"I believe it would be a good idea. We could make up for lost time that way."

"Me too. From now on we will start at six."

And so it went for the next few weeks. In the woods at six, work till six that evening. The logs were coming out in droves now and the Semi was hauling away three loads every two days. It was the first of November now and the weather turned cooler as they started on the big Walnuts. Billy was running the crawler wide open to keep up with his father and Ted. Some days he fell behind with his dragging.

"You know Dad, if we had a skidder we could get the logs out faster."

"I know son, but we can't afford to buy a skidder right now, in a couple of years but not now."

"I know," Billy agreed. "The crawler is all right, just a little slow."

Thanksgiving week, the man who owned the tract of timber came out to see how Will was getting along, reminding him of the deadline. After he left Will looked at Billy and Ted.

"If I didn't know better, I would think he wants us to fail so he can collect on that bond."

"Yeah. I think you are right about that Will, Ted replied. Didn't you talk to him when you traded for the tract?"

"No, just to the family lawyer. And he seemed to be a stickler for small details."

"Well, if nothing breaks bigger than a shoe string, we should be done by the last week of December," Ted replied.

After Thanksgiving the weather turned colder and they had to drop back to seven in the mornings on account of the shorter days, but they always worked till dark. They were all tired and worn out, but the clock was ticking right along. Will had promised a nice Christmas bonus if they were finished on time, as they all pushed theirselfs to make it. But in the first week of December there was another accident. This time Will tripped over a root carrying his big Stihl saw breaking his left arm. He turned the air blue around him cussing a blue streak. Getting himself up, he made it to the log yard where Billy was loading the Semi carrying his broken arm.

"What happened Dad," he shouted as he climbed off the loader?

"I tripped and fell on my arm. Think it's broke."

Billy helped him into the pickup rushing him to the Doctor. It was broke all right, between the elbow and wrist. Doc Smith set it, putting it in a cast for Will as he shook his head.

"I swear Will. I do believe you are accident prone."

Will sat there, a disgusted look on his face. "Yeah that's me all right, big and clumsy and dumb. What the Hell am I gonna do Doc. Can you fix me so I can at least run the crawler?"

Doc Smith shook his head. "Wish I could Will, but it is like your leg. You would do more damage than good trying to work. You would be climbing in and out of the crawler all day. You could fall and break something else."

When they got in the truck Will told Billy to drive back out to the log yard. Ted was coming out of the woods as they pulled in carrying Will's saw.

"What's happened Will," he called?

Will got out of the truck holding up his broken arm with the white cast on it.

"Knew something happened to you. I found your saw where you fell and scattered the leaves." He shook his head. I believe this tract has got a jinx on you Will."

"I begin to believe it myself Ted. First the leg and now this arm. But at least I can drive the pickup and help around the log yard a little. Could have been worse. I could have broke another leg."

Ted had to laugh at that, and Will joined him.

For the next two weeks Billy drug out the trees cutting them up into log lengths while Will stacked them. It was slow work with one hand but he managed it, only he couldn't load the log trailer. Billy had to take off from dragging long enough to load it. Will was getting discouraged and knew he was not going to make the deadline working like this. He hardly slept at night forcing himself to work every day.

Ten days were left on the contract now, he knew he was losing ground. Billy and Ted were worn to the bone, and on top of that Will had a nagging cough. Ten days before the deadline he couldn't drag his aching body out of bed He called for Billy to come into his bedroom.

"It's up to you now son. Maybe if you and Ted work all through Christmas you can make it, maybe. Give it your best shot son."

He fell back on the bed coughing and hacking. Madge was standing there and felt his forehead.

"You are burning up with fever Will. I am taking you into see Doc Smith right now."

With him helping her, she got him dressed and into the car. At Dr Smith's office he checked him over, listening to Will's labored breathing through his stethoscope, shaking his head.

"Will, I am going to put you in the hospital for a few days. You have pneumonia."

Madge got up out of her chair, giving him a worried look, "I was afraid of that."

Pore ole Will just shook his head. "After this I am going to get me a job at a filling station pumping gas.

The Doctor and his wife both laughed at that. They knew he had sawdust in his veins.

After getting Will settled into a bed at the hospital, Madge drove out to the log yard to tell Billy about his father.

"He has been pushing himself too hard Mom. Even with that broke arm, he still insisted on running the loader stacking logs."

"I know son, your father is a hard headed man, and very Independent."

"I don't think we are going to make the deadline Mom," Billy said, staring at the few logs laying there.

"Just do the best you can son, that is all any man can do."

Billy smiled at her. "I guess I am a man now Mom."

"Yes you are son." She gave him a loving look. "You are a man doing a man's work. Your father and I are very proud of you."

He grinned at her. "I love you too Mom."

Madge got back into her car and drove into Martinville to the hospital to check on Will.

The next day it was spitting snow when Billy met Ted at the log yard. The weather was cold, but not disagreeable, just good working weather. The sound of a truck coming in caught their attention.

"Too early for the Semi," Ted said looking down the road.

The smooth sound of a diesel engine filled the still morning air. A red Mack truck with the name, Pat Brady Logging Company pulled up and stopped. A big burly man dropped out of the cab, as another man opened the passenger door and hollared at them as the first man came around the front of the truck.

"Mornin' loggers!" boomed out a deep voice, "how are you doin'."

"Morning Pat, Mike" Billy and Ted called out.

Pat Brady and his son Mike came over to shake their hands.

"We heard you boys was in a bind," Pat said, so we come to help you out."

Billy was flabbergasted at that. "I thought you were tied up Pat."

"We got done three days ago, an' when we heard about Will and his bad luck, we thought you could use some help. We ain't the only ones either. Jack Miller an' his boys will be here soon, along with Sam Cook an' his brother Ed. Just then two more trucks pulled in, one of them hauling a Timber Jack skidder and the other one a Case W-14 loader. All the trucks carried Stihl chain saws on them. Pat had driven his tractor with the log trailer hooked to it. The men all gathered around Billy and Ted, ready to go to work.

"I don't, quite know what to say," Billy told them.

"Don't have to say nothin' Billy," Pat spoke up. "Your father has helped every one of us at one time or another an' never asked for anything back. Now he is in the hospital flat of his back an' the timber has to be out an' done by the end of this month an' by Hell we are goin' to help you get it out!"

Billy's chest swelled with pride as he looked at the men around him. They stood there eager to help him and Ted finish the tract, to pull the fat out of the fire for his father. He felt a deep kinship with them, these hard working men of the woods, these fellers of timber, these brother loggers.

"Well son, give us our orders," Pat laughed.

Billy grinned at him. "You know what needs to be done Pat, we need to get them Walnuts out."

"All right boys," Pat called, "let's get to it."

Soon the woods resounded to the snarl of chain saws and the bellow of diesel engines lugging. Logs began to pile up in the log yard. Mike Brady loaded their log trailer while he waited for the other one to pull in. As soon as it was loaded, Mike followed him out and to the sawmill. The men worked like Beavers in the light spitting snow. Every day was as the last one. The men paid no attention to the weather. It was turning a little colder, but Pat said there wouldn'd be any bad weather until after the first of the year. It was too cold to rain, so they had no worrys about wet ground to hinder them. Christmas Eve came and they worked a half day dragging out what was on the ground, and stacking it.

Will sat in his easy chair watching the logs burn in the rock fireplace, smelling the good smells drifting in out of the kitchen where Madge was preparing Christmas dinner. Billy lay on the couch watching T-V, and napping. Will knew he was worn out from the hectic pace he had been setting. He thought of his good friends who had pitched in to help him out of a bad situation. Pat told him it would take at least four more days to finish up, and Will prayed for clear weather. Madge glanced in at him from time to time, seeing him sitting there staring into the fire as it danced throwing out it's cheery glow. Will was thankful for his family and friends as his thoughts revolved around the things that had happened over the last seven months.

Next morning after Christmas Day at daylight the men converged upon the remaining Walnut trees left on the tract. They had five days left and were pushing hard to make it. The man buying the logs sent in another truck to help keep the log yard cleared out, because the men were pouring the logs into it. On the fourth day, Pat Brady came out with his big Stihl cut down saw over his shoulder, a wide grin on his face.

"Well Billy, I just dropped the last tree of the lot. Before dark every log should be loaded an' on the way to the mill!"

Billy took off his cap and threw it into the air, "Whoooeee," he yelled.

Pat stood laughing, lighting one of his foul smelling cigars. "Yes sir. We got it licked. We got the bear by the tail in a downhill drag by Gar!"

Before it got dark, all the machinery was loaded and heading out. Billy tried to express his thanks to the men, but they waved him off. Your Daddy would have done the same for any one of us he was told.

"You tell Will, we will be looking for a new year's drink from him," Pat said.

"You bet I'll tell him,' Billy laughed.

The next morning at ten o'clock Billy drove Will out to the big lumber and veneer mill of Lawton Industries where they met with the lawyer for the family that owned the land where the timber was cut.

"Well Mr Thurman, I see you made your deadline," the lawyer told him.

"With the help of my son here, some good friends and the grace of God."

The thin faced lawyer smiled a thin smile. "Yes, I see. Now for the paper work."

When it was all settled up, Will had a good sized check that brought a smile to his face. The bond check was returned to him and as he stood to leave, the lawyer stuck out his hand. Grinning, Will took it.

"I want you to know Mr Thurman, having you sign a bond was not my idea. But, the family I work for are an untrusting sort. So I have to go along with their wishes. I have heard nothing but good things about you and knew you were a man to be trusted, as one can tell by your many friends."

"Thank you Mr Wilson. Pleasure doing business with you."

Billy and Will left the office and headed for the bank to deposit the check. Clark Gray met them at his office door.

"Well Will, I see you made it, and with a day to spare."

"Yeah, we did. But I still don't know how Pat and the others knew about me so quick. They were there the day after I was put in the hospital."

"Oh that. You see I knew you needed help. They were all done for the winter, so I spread the word and they answered the call."

"I'll be dammed. You did that?"

"It wasn't hard. After they found out what was going on, everybody just pitched in. After all, what are friends for if you don't use them once in a while."

Will threw back his head and roared with laughter. After he settled down he looked across the desk at Clark.

"I may never have much in the way of riches, but I am rich in friends and that is better than anything money can buy!"

New Year's Eve, a big party was in full swing at Will and Madge's home with all the men who helped him get the timber out there. Pat and Mike Brady and their wife's, the Cooke brothers and their wife's, Jack Miller with his wife and daughter Ann, who was Billy's age and his two sons along with Ted, his wife, Clark Gray and his wife There were good eats, lively conversation, dancing and plenty of good cheer toasts. Outside snowflakes were falling, but inside there was the warmth of good friends and companionship. Whatever the New Year might bring, nothing would ever dampen the spirits of those inside on this New Year's Eve. Hard times had brought them together, and hard times had made a man out of a sixteen year old boy who had put his shoulder to the wheel working against all odds to help his Mother and Father.

THE END